DREAMING BIG

By

JETT JAMES

Table of Contents

The Dedication

This book is dedicated to Momma B. Big B, Balinda L. When the time has shown to be not so nice, the holy spirit in this woman reaches out to the depth of an individual's soul, to be honest, and sincere. A humbling the advice that is provided and the time that she takes to encourage and help those whom she cares for and sees a need that she can help. Everyone has a character that makes them who they have grown from long ago, like when she made her first tuna fish and the many times of laughter and serious conversation. You are a person to me thateveryone could stand to have. You don't have to speak every day, you do not need to text or calldaily, weekly or monthly. However, in times of need, she is always right on time. Thank youfor always standing in the gap and supporting me in the lonely times and showing me that life is about more than me. From the life-saving advice you provided for me, I see the joy in my babies and their babies and I am here to enjoy seeing their growth and development. Get you a Momma B, an honest friend that I will always be grateful for and appreciate for not following the crowd and standing on who we are in our personal relationship in the small space that we occupy when we occupy. God will identify those who are true friends and to me, you are that. I dedicate this book to you.
Dreaming Big!

Her Story

Theme:

Her Story - Dreaming Big

Characters:

Storytellers:

Jett

Jett James

Prelude:

Should've seen it coming the trajectory of life spiraling through death and destruction, the road to bad choices and long nights. The growth of wisdom and experience. The toasting to learning life the hard way.

I was off to college in spite of having a baby. I was still favoured enough to get to go to the Business Technology School that I chose. I passed all of the entrance exams, qualified forhousing and off to begin my life as a college student. I received help from my cousin with my baby so I could concentrate on my learnings until I got settled. I am full of excitement and expectation. The next step to my future. My college experience.

Then it happened. I wasn't home sick but I had a baby whom I loved so every weekend Iwould find myself back in my hometown, Fremont. Choices had to be made, so I decided to get an apartment so I could have my baby close. A cousin helped me secure an apartment and daycare as I pursued my college journey.

Yep, Enter Him. The man that will walk with me from a girl to a wife. The man who willintroduce me to the woman I could be and shouldn't be. I was Her.

Here is me looking at what it took to get me here. The journey, the twists and turns of life, the ups and downs of choices and consequences. The reality of the environments we allow ourselves and our children to grow up in. The trauma that we imply in the selfishness of living insin thinking it's the good life. The growth of seeing yourself for who you really are and taking thesteps to change the things about yourself that you do not like. She is looking back and seeing the favor and hand of God through every test and trial preparing you for the glory of today.

Walking where you can not see in order to see, takes faith and

2

determination.

Dedication and humbleness, the willingness to learn and the eye to discern. Life is a journey, you can live it or you can survive it. How you trot through it is up to your perception. At the endof the line, it will be you standing there reviewing the events of your life that make you. Will you like what you see? Can you stand before God and scroll through all of the things you thought were done in the dark? Have you emptied out your closet of the secret sins that you are ashamed of? God knows, have you asked for forgiveness? Have you forgiven yourself?

Perspective the outlook you have on life will help you walk out the rest of your days.

Some days will be better than others, nevertheless, each day is yours to make it better than theday before.

Chapter 1 Meeting Him

Look! Stop telling people that I am fucking you! I have never touched you and everyone in town is telling me that we are sleeping together. She responded in a shy flirty laugh." I did notsay that... I don't know where they got that from." He responded sternly that they got that from you.

I sat watching not knowing even If I believed her and she was my bestie. She is known for just lying, lying to just tell a lie. I call it unnecessarily lying because it is not even necessary. As this exchange is happening they soon come to the conclusion the person she thought was him was actually his brother who gave her the wrong name and she is bragging about someone that she doesn't even know. Shaking my head.

Soon the attention was directed at me due to I had not been introduced to this sexy built man. His shoulders were broad and wide on his slender body with the ribbed six-pack glistening as his shirt blew against his body. He smelled of cologne and hairline to a crisp. Though this man is speaking to my loins, I am not interested. As I responded to his many questions, I decided I had no interest so I am not going to put on any representative. I am just going to be me. And that is where it all started.

Finally! At the right spot at the right time. My childhood friend is now throwing all of the after parties at his place and it is next door to my house. No more drunk driving, I can park and walk home. Nice! These parties were the best. Everyone who was anyone was at these parties, the DJ was on point, that click and they click holding up the walls. That was not us, we were the ones who came in and went to the dance floor and danced the night away, we could have fun all by ourselves so you might well join. We got our drink on and some got their smoke on. They were doing business over there and they were shooting dice right here. All the guys were scoping who they were going to take to a room and creep with and all the girls were waiting to get chosen. I had a man, well half of a man. I had a boyfriend but he decided to go on the run and then I had someone else boyfriend on the side. Just so happened once I decided to be single. My side dude must have thought that I wanted him to be my main man... Which was not the case. So he advised me to get a new boyfriend.

The very next day the dude asked if he could take me and my daughter to the beach. I finally said yes. We went shopping for beach toys and clothing and then spent the day at the beach. Once we finished at the beach we went to the park for some parking lot pimping. It was there when I introduced my side dude to my new dude. Hi boyfriend B, meet my new boyfriend A. and that is when this journey began.

I don't know if the text was to tell me or to just dig in and hurt me. The timing of the news of the gathering of all family except me on my Birthday. You're my mother of course you knew this.

When you told me you meant it as a dig. It is so apparent. If you didn't mean it maliciously youwould've told me it was on my birthday. You just said April, but you slipped up when you informed my daughter. Your mean. Just mean. My family is a representative of a bunch of people who do not like each other but their hatred of me binds them more than any real beef they have within themselves. No, I am not perfect and I have made mistakes, so have all of them. What makes me stand out? What makes me the enemy? I just want to love and show love. Is that too much to ask? Where do I go from here?

Breaking generational curses is not easy. It comes with a price. The things that you have doneto me, you will not have the chance to do to my children's children. It stops here. I need to create my own vision of life and how I see it and leave all those who do not care or love me. I need to leave them where they are. Time to Dream Big, Dream

5

Big by myself because you canclap and help every chance you get, in the end, no one is cheering with you or for you. The realities of life.

Public relationship vs Personal relationship

Many people live their lives in the public eye. You don't have to be rich and famous, but they are included too. We are now in an age of likes and shares, streaming and influence. It is called reality yet it is scripted. Then they find observers of a culture to influence a culture to be like them or comfort them with what is cool and what is not. Thus making relationships public and for others' views. I love this person now for how it looks and what it can do for me, not so much of me and you against the world for richer or poor, sickness and health. Divorce is due to more of a financial increase than broken heart irreconcilable differences. Adultery is at an all-time high and now people are convinced that it is the thing to do, have multiple partners and share your partners. That is a public agreement inside of what should be a personal relationship. No judgment, just defining the difference between a personal and public relationship.

In a public relationship, all eyes are on you. Your steps are reported in the media through word of mouth. All of the actions are on display, the fights, the gifts, the children, the wedding, the parties, the extra people involved in the relationship. People are always around to tell your story to the next person who will listen. You will find others desiring what you have and others say Girl I would never. When you are in your early 20's you have many public relationships.

I really did not know what to expect once I rang the bell and can confidently state that I have overcome, conquered, and touched the hem of His garment. I know I am in His hands and He is my healer, my provider, my friend. I did it, we did it, I could've never made it without Him on my side. He is my everything, I love Him with my whole heart and my whole soul.

OH, you trying to be funny, you want me to go get a man? Did you ever think I was ok with just being with you, even though you had someone? I was young going to college and beginning my life. I like you, but what we have was really just physical. You introduced my body to things it had never known before and I liked it. It wasn't much more, I still lived at home with my mom. Two can play that game, The Dude has been asking me to go out with him for weeks, and today I will say yes. It was a beach date and of course, my daughter and I had nothing to wear. It is one of the only times I remember going to Walmart on the east side. Being the smart ass I am, he treated me so we could go on the date, so I bought bathing suits and hats. I also loaded the cart with every beach toy that Walmart had to offer for the age of my baby girl. He paid willingly, so it was. We enjoyed the day at the beach on our first date, and once going home and changing we met up atthe park and I had the opportunity to introduce my side dude to my new Dude. My poor BFF didn't know what to do or what to say. Sometimes I had to just spring on her because her reaction always has everybody laughing and they forget what I just did. Yeah, your girl was savage, I did not realize so much back then, but looking back ...lol.

The relationship started off shaky. I just agreed to be his girl because my side dude told me to get a boyfriend. It was many days of my Dude coming to get me from my friend's house that I was there with my side dude. I finally gave in and told him after this weekend of being with him Iwould be his girlfriend. Savage, Did I mention I may have been savage?

So I did as I said and spent some time with my new Dude. That is my Dude and we are a "couple". This man put something on me that night. Things I had never experienced prior to sleeping beside him. The first night we stayed together, I don't know if I fell in love but I did take his money and went to my college apartment that was located two hours away. It was the first time I had done anything like that, but after that night of love making. Whew, I should have been paid for the voodoo he put on me. Savage wink wink.

He wasn't mad when he found out that I had left, he never even mentioned the money to this day. He had to know it was me. I left early in the morning and I left town. Go figure. My cousin and I had travelled down to my college town just for a weekend getaway, I did just take this guy's money. SMH Wouldn't you know it, there was something in store for me. He called and asked me to come back and go to a party with him later that night. Wouldn't you know it, two hours later I wasback in my hometown with my new dude. Of course, he was seeing other girls prior to our announcement and as I was sitting next to him smiling feeling all giggly thinking about the feeling later tonight, this heffa spilt a beer on me! I had to laugh it off cause I knew why she was mad, however, I got that ass back a few years later. Patience is a virtue. Savage.

He bought me gifts and we dressed alike at parties. We held hands and hung around each other when we were out. He had a nickname for me, he was the man. Everyone knew him, they were building their empire and I was a queen in the kingdom. It was a very public relationship, he showered me with gold and clothes. It even advanced into houses and cars. That man provided and spoiled me, but the public display of affection also was a public display of disrespect, cheating, stress and relationship issues I had never experienced or seen.A public display that used to have me talking to God explaining that I was not experiencing these things for no reason. That God had a purpose for all things that drove me absolutely crazy in this season of my life.

When you have the right perspective, you can stay in faith even when life is not fair. You canmove forward even when you should be stuck.

The first time he hit me it took me by surprise. I had grown up an only child in a single-parent home, my whole life so the family experience I did not have. I was a loner and did not speak with my mother at all besides her telling me to get up for school or for me to come to wash the dishes. I did receive everything I asked for as a youth, played

8

sports during school and kept busy and gone. Every summer I went off to another relative's house to spend the summer to experience a bondwith family.

We were driving down the street and we were arguing about something, most likely where and who he had been. I'm in love now, dude whipped me in the worst of ways... So we probably were arguing about him cheating or something.. He was a hoe. Well as I was driving to take him to his house, he reached over and punched me in my face as I came to a stop at thestop sign. This Nigga done lost his mind, I had never been hit before not even really in a fight so of course it took no time for me to react. I didn't even place the car in park as my foot lifted off of the break and the car began to roll. I was out of the driver's seat on top of him hitting him back and letting him know this is not that! I got his ass! Put his hands on me, I am not his child!

Joker! Savage, I say Savage. Let me tell you how this worked out. So once he saw I was not having it and he had now given me a black eye, I had to go home and face my mother, who hadmy child. So we cooled down from the fight to go get my baby, he went in with me because he wanted to explain to my mother. As a man, he walks into the house and asks to speak to my mother. He then stated to her that He had hit me and left a bruise on my face, he was apologetic and wanted to be a man and tell her himself. You know that comeback made him think about things, in my mind. However, my mother's response is something that I will never forget and took me years to get past. She stated without hesitation, that she probably deserved it. Did she deserve it? Who responds that way, and whose mother accepts that for their only daughter? I was devastated, I thought for many years after she stated I deserved it that I did, so I spent thenext 10 or so years thinking I deserved the beatings I was receiving. A public display of embarrassment.

Things were just an up-and-down roller coaster, I would be showered with gifts in front of my friends and every girl in town, gold, flowers,

9

and clothes. I was shopping so much, I did not want to shop any more. I had so much gold I started buying my friends gold rings and watches. I paid for the drinks and was always sure to provide the entertainment for the night. My relationship was public. As he was seeing other people after my mental heartbreak breakdown, I began living my own life as well. I would only respond to not being responded to for he was busy or not worried about me until someone told him I was out. It became so routine that I began to prepare for the nightly entertainment. My relationship was public.

His routine was to wait until I was out and then he would come and get me, start a fight so I would go home or he would try to send me home so he could be with someone else that evening. This process consisted of an argument, a fight, him telling me to take off the clothes he bought, and me having to go home to change cause he ripped my shirt or took my shoes. Me being savage as I am... Figured out the play.

Fool me once shame on you, fool me twice cannot be fooled again - George Bush.

I prepared this time, it was not going to happen, I had some side plans so my BFF and I just prepared for the evening. I was casually drinking and having fun with my BFF and the potential friends for the night. We figured out the routine so we made a schedule. She knew what to do. When my dude came into the bar, the fight. I advised my BFF to tell my later friend to just chill and watch the show. Dude and I argued, and then we had to leave, he hit me a couple of times, took me back to the bar, and proceeded to try to take my clothes that he bought. By this time, my hair is messed up and now you're taking me out of my clothes. I was smart. So the bar is crowded by this time and the dude is trying his best but I don't budge. I have something to do, I am not leaving so go on and do what you want. He was so pissed, as I took off the shirt he purchased and handed it to him standing in the parking lot in a tank top, I knew this was happening, my BFF hands me another shirt she pulls from the trunk. Prepared.

As far as the hair, The new friend loaned me his hat so we could continue with our night. I finished the night with no shoes on, but we were sitting so anyone hardly even noticed. The main event of that night was when my dude was trying to get at me and he ran on top of all of the cars in the parking lot. It's funny reflecting at the time it was not, all I could hear was my BFF saying "Run Bitch Run, don't just stand there" but it was a funny sight to see him running across those cars and nobody saying anything. A public relationship.

This relationship was so public that when the girls he would cheat on me with would get pregnant they would come and tell me. My response I remember one time was "Why are you telling me, I did not sleep with you". It was not my business. You slept with my Dude and got pregnant now he won't answer your calls, that's personal. Yet, I was sure to deliver the message.

I went through almost 20 years of drama. Stress and drama. He would cheat on me, have babies and then defend our relationship to the end. It was really crazy. I had to challenge myself to stay with this man for a whole year. Whew when that year was up, I took a day off of work to move out. There was nothing wrong but my year's challenge was up. Our relationship was up and down and the whole town was a part of it.

There were many situations that involved questions, guns, fights and make-up sex. We ran, we hid, we laughed, we argued. This was the life, we were living. It was a lot of parting, a lot of drinking, a lot of sex. There was the time my Dude came crying in a blue jean fringe jacket.

Yes, Mexican style. A strong-built black man in this girly fringe blue jean coat, again that conversation ended with my BFF saying ' Run Bitch Run"... He was going to shoot her too, I think. There were times I would wake in one man's arms while my dude stood over us as we slept, with a gun. There were times when we had to sneak out of parties to go and do something so he would not know what I was doing or whom I was doing it with. There were times when I picked up other guys in his car or times when I would go work the door at my Dude's club to get the money to go to the competition's club. Savage. But to my defence, he was glad I was gone, he did his thing.

At one time we had split and I had dated another fella for over a year and a half. Nevertheless, my Dude decided to fake his way out of the county jail and shoot my fella, who at the time was at another girl's house, as he left her house my dude shot the fella's car up as he turned the corner. He was arrogant, he was cocky. I guess he thought If he couldn't cheat on me no one could. My fella spent a week or more in the ICU unit. What a story that was in his hometown. This relationship now has passed from the North to the South. A Public relationship. This led to newspaper articles, attempted murder charges, facing 11 to 25 years court case, and murder Of course they put that all stemmed from a girl. Savage. SMH.

We, my dude and I have a growing baby, and in spite of everything I do not want her to grow up without her father. Time has passed and this is a weird season for me. No one seems to understand the quandary that I have myself in, my man and my child's father. Guns, attempted murder, double-digit jail time. And the females I knew thought it was cute. It was a time of isolation for me because I did not know what to do, think, expect or pray. I walked into that courtroom strong with my head held high in the baddest white jean-fitted dress. (I love that dress, only wore it that one time.) I went in open and came to the attention of my Dude. He still loved me, all charges had been dropped.

Murder, the weeks leading up to the court case had my fella needing to come and testify the grand jury had already issued the indictment with the evidence they had and the witness statement. While waiting for trial, my fella was gunned down in an alley in College Park GA. That day that incident changed my life forever. Murder, the man I loved lay murdered in a dark alley.

Strength and honour are her clothing: And she shall rejoice in time to come. She openeth hermouth with wisdom; And in her tongue is the law of Kindness

Proverbs 31: 25-26

I want an office building with offices according to the structure of the business that is built on solid ground. The development is run out of one headquarters with family on the board of directors making sure that each business is operating effectively and efficiently with customer service and kindness that exceeds the expectations of the people enjoying their jobs and working towards their goals. I would like to build a business based on the principles that wehave shared with the world. The impact of our program has affected the infrastructure of the world and encouraged a new generation of leaders and managers who lead with kindness and manage with courage as they are working with the lord. Jesus keeps us humble in the blessings bestowed upon us. Let us be lenders and not borrowers, Let us be forgiving and wise. I want this business to give God the glory. My God the God that provided his son so we can be saved. Let us always be able to spot the Judas and be able to shield ourselves with thelove and kindness of the Holy Spirit. That evil lives are changed and they seek the kingdom of peace and joy. In Jesus name, I pray. Amen.

I walked in with amazement this place was more beautiful than I imagined. When they say Godwill show up and show out this has to be what they meant. I did not dream this big. This is mine, well ours, God is in everything! He is amazing.

The floors glisten in the sunlight and the furniture has soft leather like in a Bentley or rolls, the color is poppin' and the tables are exquisite with high-class taste. It makes you not want to touch anything yet so welcoming to just experience. You sit and you aspire for more,

13

people are inspired just to work towards their best, their top tier, making their big dreams come true. In the middle is a prominent photo of AP.. my cousin, best friend, and big sister... The way her lips perk out and her blonde hair standing, she says Go You!! Umm Huh, you look good, you got this. It is okay to be you!!

The energy is felt when you walk in, you are greeted with a smile and can access tea, coffee, or cold lemon cucumber water. Hi welcome to the Celeb, how may we assist you today? The faint sound of gospel music during the first few hours of the day. We are going to get our praises on a daily basis, this is how we start as a team, praising our way through to make this day great!!

Marketing controls the marketing and finance reports on all finances that are split within the company. Equity in the company equates to the voting power that a person has. This is my business. I own 60% of everything. God has full control and the ultimate say in the direction ofeach department.

The success and profitability of a nonprofit company are complex, however, we stay focused on the details so we are operating efficiently and effectively to be able to branch out and provide opportunities to a number of small businesses that help support the infrastructures of any given community. I said I was scared, scared not of fear or horror but scared of the success, scared of how to manage and manoeuvre the next level of advancement in life. Who walks with you, will you have to walk alone? Scared of the security that you have developed in knowing who you are and what you want out of life. Your direction, your wisdom, your knowledge, the path that was laid for you for a time such as this. Walking boldly in knowing who you are and that you areloved, that you are strong, that you are wise, that you can do all things through Christ who strengthens you. That God made you for a purpose and you are walking in it. Scared - thrown into or being in a state of fear, fright or panic. My fear, or fright is of success. I am going to face it head-on. God did not bring me this far to leave me. Now look at all of my

14

dreams, goals and desires standing before me in a business that God placed on my heart years ago and developed me and continues to develop me until His will is done. Each day I ask for strength and protection of the infrastructure of a people. My people, your people, all people.

I walked into the room with butterflies in my stomach yet the glow of confidence, the strut of purpose and the grace of an angel.I God had brought me here and I know Jesus loves me.

The people's eyes shifted and expectation and humbleness took over the room. We all were looking forward to the opportunity of fellowship.

My life changed after that, that is when I knew my life changed. Looking back, I saw the pattern and the preparation for the most important relationship I would ever have. It was the introduction or continuation of a relationship I was Chosen to have before I was born. My mother stated that I was born on a Stormy Easter Sunday. Obstacles stood in her way to get to the hospital, she endured physical pain, mental pain, spiritual anguish and just plain heartbreak. She was home alone, her sisters who were there let the evil in their spirit take over and walked out even though their sister sat yelling in pain. Not until her mother came home did she get to the hospital, still then she had to endure people taking their time and showing no concern for prevailing pain. As they travelled to the hospital just a few miles away, tornado-like winds stirred up, large puddles accumulated in the streets, and power lines fell multiple times bringing the car to sudden stops, twists and turns. Finally, she arrived and I was brought into the world. The favour my life from this journey my mother travelled, showed favour from those classmates, andfriends that she had. Her influence favoured me to advance in my career and my dream home from the favour placed on me in knowing the right people at the right time. Thanks to my mother, for not giving up on bringing me into this world.

The weight of walking into the unknown. I learned a very important lesson in this season of my journey. There is power in your thoughts. Have you ever wondered or even paid attention to the fact what you think about daily what you work on daily or what is on your mind all of the time, whether good or bad? Enough thought and enough time and mostly enough belief it comes to pass? You see yourself winning that race, you see yourself in a relationship with that person, you see yourself with that job or vehicle and you actually receive it. The thing is this doesn't just happen to me or you but all of us have experienced this. You just have to look deep enough and be honest with yourself to see the pattern in your thoughts and perspective to results and execution. How many times have you thought your partner was cheating etc. you believe it to the point where you seek it out? At that point don't be surprised when you find what you're looking for. It may not be your fault, but you wouldn't have found it if you didn't go looking. It's two sides to that analogy, don't get it twisted, but see the point I am trying to make. The perspective of thoughts matters.

A co-worker had lost her husband and I was there to see the pain and revelation on her face, to see how she worked in her pain with tears rolling down her face. Due to us working 7 days per week 12 hours per day, I had nothing to do but think.

I thought about what it would be like to lose someone close to me. At this point in life, the only people I knew to die were old people who lived a good life. I thought if I lost my boyfriend, who at the time had just called me on Sunday to say that no matter what exact words "No BS, no matter what happens I will see you next Saturday." That next Saturday I was standing over him in his casket 1800 miles away from my small town home. I had thought about losing him the whole week prior, putting myself in my co-worker's shoes, processing emotions and plans etc. implanting my own scenario. I thought and thought I received the call from Him on Sunday, while at work on Monday after bragging and showing my excitement that he will be back to me this week, my co-worker's friend called to inform me that my fella had been Murdered in GA. This was real, I felt the shock go through my body, this was real. Tears just flow, my heart has broken. I have thought this into existence.

God prepared me more equipped for this pain, for it would change the course of my life forever. Changed the way I think.

The process of grieving is different for each individual. I know people learn of the stages and it is important to know where you are in the process so you can work towards processing and living with your grief. My grief was so heavy I am positive I had a nervous breakdown, consciously but uncontrolled. I was at work and every time I crossed the safety line I would burst into tears, real uncontrollable tears. I did not understand. I floated through the services and attempted to proceed with life like all my plans and future were not just ripped from me. I was covering my true emotions hiding behind a fake smile, like it meant nothing when it meant everything. It was heavy, it got too heavy and work, drinking and denial were not helping. I was weak, I could not withstand it anymore. Something had to give. I'm a curious person so I tested it with my co-worker friend who had told me of his death in the first place. He stood and watched as I would be fine and soon as I crossed the line my emotions were out of control. I called my BFF and her mother made me an appointment with a counsellor the very next day. Of course, I was unable to work, so we had to figure this out.

I attended one session with the counsellor in person and a couple on the phone to report my progress. Sometimes we just need direction to know how to heal, we have to be humble enough to ask for help. It took me up to three years to fully grieve, During this time I learned lessons like not making lifetime decisions when you are hurting and taking the time to heal and understand who and where you are in life. This will allow you to set a path to the life you desire and that was proposed for you. Walking where you can't see in order to see.

This is still a very public relationship, everyone is watching, they watched when my dude, now my child's father, shot my fella as he left another girl's home. My dude, Child Father turned himself in and at the time of my fella's murder, my dude was indicted by the grand jury for my fella'sattempted murder. Mind you I am still grieving, now even more confused and stressed, this is my child's father, her dad. He is a good dad, just a little crazy and thinks he owns me. So in this confused state, what do I do at this point in life? Get back with him and marry him. Yes, less than a year from my fella's murder. These are the choices that were made in my grief when I was trusting the Lord because I had no direction. I was numb just existing. I needed the Lord to be in control because I was too weak. I know now God has a purpose in everything. I was married to my child's father for two years. In those two years, God showed up, showed purpose and the season that we were in needed to happen the way it did. It was my path of life. Difficult as it was, how everyone watched makes it much easier to share and be transparent.

Everyone watched it and saw it like it was the Cosby show in the 90's on Thursdays at 8 PM. I learned everything happens for a reason. In the short time before we were married, we went to court for battery, we moved in together, we worked jobs, we took care of our family, and he made other babies. I floated and just went with the flow, there was cheating on both sides. I did say I was savage right?

Our wedding was held on a beautiful Saturday afternoon in August. My aunt helped me plan and execute a beautiful setup for us in her yard. The chairs, the arch and the tent were set perfectly. White limos lined the street followed by white Cadillacs. Twelve bridesmaids, two flower girls, a miniature bride and all the gents to go along, it was a very large wedding. Black long dresses each to the individual style tux to match, and the white chairs and red roses to accent showed a beautiful display. The traffic rounded the corner all afternoon with people just stopping to join the party. I cried as I walked down that Isle alone, but I wasn't alone. God had given me the direction to marry this man, and I trusted him so I walked uprightly and boldly knowing I was doing his will and he was with me. The Lord has always protected and providedfor me and for that I am grateful.

We finished the night at the nightclub my now husband owned, providing a celebration for the whole town to enjoy from the afternoon to the wee hours of the morning. We ended our wedding night at Denny's and then home. The next year would produce situations like burning my sister-in-law and helping with her son, cursing my brother-in-law, moving into unknown areas and ending back home with my mother, moving to a place I never wanted to be to only move 3 months later 1600 miles away without telling anyone until 3 days later. I'm in Texas with my husband, a sacrifice I will make because my daughter wants her father. I love my children and looking back I am grateful and thankful for all the sacrifices I made just for them. During this time I am still in grief. So just went with the flow. I was not myself. I was living in a shell of myself, and trusting God got me through, even if it was not always easy. The things I have been through helped me become the person I am today. I like her so it was not in vain.

In thinking about manifesting your thoughts, in the meantime the 3 months I was living where I never wanted to. I was trusting God so much I would wake up each morning and get dressed for the office job that I always wanted. I wanted to work from 9 to 5 Monday through Friday. I wanted to work in an office building that was beautiful and had phones, computers etc. I was detailed. So I woke up each day and went into my kitchen like I had work and I worked on my business plan that continued to be developed till this day. Dreaming Big. My relationship with my husband had fallen apart pretty much and he left and went to Texas and I was left with the friends from the union who knew I had pretty much lost my mind. They sat and watched as I dressed up and "went to work" in my kitchen. Not saying a word just watching and suggesting things for me to work on, I know they thought I was crazy, I was in a way. At five o'clock I would change my clothes and continue my day as if I

19

am home from work.

Kinda ironic as I see the state of the world after 2020 where I am now working from home, like I always wanted and the consistency of my dressing and working allowed me to finda job within two weeks of being in Texas at the largest building on the island. I thought and worked for what I wanted and it came to pass, even when I was in the wilderness.

While in Texas, I faced many giants, jail, fights, stolen cars, moving, in-laws disrespect, not knowing anyone, children's services, no water, no lights, no food, no transportation, many days of just praying and being lost. In the wilderness.

As you look back and reflect, I was never alone. There was always someone to provide it was my sister-in-law who was leaving the family as well, the food pantry that provided nutrients for that day, or my mother who kept my children for a year to get me together. Or the man that God brought into my life so I would not be alone who would later serve a purpose for me to return back north for the sacrifice for my other daughter to be close to her father. I often think I was not supposed to marry him, but everything happens for a reason and it would have been more difficult to make it back up north without him. The giant and the evil that we had to face with that man cost me a relationship with my daughter and activities that would change our lives forever. We are much better people for surviving what we have been through, we hope to use it to heal others and that may be why God allowed it to happen to us. We conquer and we learn from our mistakes and we look unto the Father for understanding, somethings are natural, but know and seek the supernatural. You are equipped for what you are called for, not everything feels good. God will get the glory in the end if your purpose is pure.

So while in Texas I finally tricked my then-husband, my dude, into giving me a divorce not willingly. However, after he put me in jail, it was easy to file for divorce and once the attorney general pulled information from our "incidents" in my home town and the news articles and attempted murder it was easy to get a restraining order on him for the next five years of my life not to be within 100 ft. The fact the federal government was already seeking him out and provided a seven-year vacation allowed me to get a life per se. Once my divorce was final, why, oh why did I rush and get married again? I married a man that I had only known for 6 months and I was still in my grief time. Still not myself, I was just existing. This guy, he was a nice man, a little slow and he tricked me with the word of the Lord, he knew it, however never grew at that time with it. I am a mover and eventually, I was going to have the strength to start fighting again.

When my strength came back he was not prepared, even though I told him, nor was he equipped to control a woman like me. Besides, the incident with my child left him with no respect and no trust. I am not cold-hearted, as I began to get back in tune with my strength and goals we grew apart, he wanted to play with dogs, and I wanted to play with jobs.

When we came back up north, we spent months in a homeless shelter, it was church work and home for two years. Through the mountains, God made a path to a great job and security, giving back everything that was lost. In the end, we had two homes, I lived with my children in one and he lived with his dogs in the other. After the fourth month of not seeing him, I guess I should not have been surprised that he was sleeping with another woman. I really didn't care. I did say I was savage.

This book is about dreaming big and I am providing some of my history to let you in on it was the things that I have been through that have led me on the journey to my purpose, to my Big dream. Dreams derive from real life and the connections are constrained by unconscious desires hence " a dream is the fulfilment of a wish". According to Freud, dreams are the imagery of a wish or impulse that has since been repressed. At almost half a century old I have the realization and the experience to see what has helped and guided me through.

Managing your life and the experiences of your life is important. Who you trust, who you confide in and what you believe matters. Many people see dreams as tangible things that can be touched, bought and sold. Dreams are much more than that. A dream has to do with who you are, and who you see you can be, and become. That is when your young children aspire to be teachers, doctors, lawyers and politicians. Children desire to be wives, mothers and friends, Dads, husbands and uncles. The dreams of your innocents, where you dreamed to be a junkie and a street walker were absurd because you believed so much more. As children open and pure, having a village around you to encourage and protect you so you can enjoy your youth.

We began to grow up too fast, we wanted fast cars and video vixens, and we wanted the riches quickly without taking the stairs. A generation began taking care of their parents and in arrogance became disrespectful. In providing we changed roles, where the children are making the rules and not learning from their elders. We began to walk more naturally and stopped teaching the supernatural. There is good and evil, there is black and white, let your yes be yes and your no be no. In this day and age, there is very little time for doubt, walk in your vision,and work to make it come to pass. Dream Big.

Who am I and What do I want?

I had this charm for my necklace that said I want I want I want. I don't know if I bought it or my mother purchased it. At one season of my life, it was all about me. As I think back I probably owe my BFF a hug and thank you. I talked about myself so much that thinking about it is getting on my nerves. I think it is a season we all may see at one point in our lives. It is a season of learning to love yourself or in my case not loving yourself enough and looking for outside approval or input to dictate my life. I know I am not the only one, I am just admitting it. I had relationship issues family issues, and worked hard so financial issues were not an issue but how I spent and saved was terrible. No one talked to us about credit. When you start making more money than your elder family, key information is sometimes kept to themselves. For example 401 K Retirement Plan - important. Paying Taxes, and filing taxes - more important than getting a return. The trick of the government to control you, HUD, child support, WIC - what the black panthers created to help feed the poverty community was used the worst against the family.

Unless you put the child's father on child support you can not receive the benefit of WIC, yet it is not that strict with government assistance, food stamps, medical and sometimes cash assistance. Well, at least in "my day". I am an OG now... Lol

As I began to work I realized I could make $247 per month with some food stamps that lasted longer than when I made $247 per week. Crazy to look at that. I was blessed with an increase,however with no knowledge of managing it. Paying bills on time, creating credit and building it, is not a discussion in many households unless they are showing off, who is sharing how to do it or that it is important. We had money, cash not growing interest, not investing it or saving it.

That was a lesson all of us OG should share.

What is it that I really want? Where is my peace and my joy? I seek a home, a partnership, a team that works together to achieve our personal goals. The things we decide together with the guidance of our God, to show us the way. Walking by faith and not by sight. Building a family, building our family as we see fit. Allowing the flow of good vibes support and encouragement, noticing our Judas and loving them through their greed, pain and jealousy. Walking is an example of a successful relationship, between mentors, and faith walkers. Love is felt more than seen.

Respect is given and earned each day, we share our faults so we can become better, our communication and understanding are unmatched, and our peace is unexplained. This is us. This is the big dream. We build our homes as we see fit. We purchase land, and this is ours to do as we will. Access to us is not common but when you're in the presence you feel the warmth of the Holy Spirit. We work daily to walk according to His will, as men and women of God. Our children are blessed and our children's children are blessed.

Dreaming big does not always contain material physical things, it can be that inner best you, it can be your peace, the simple things of life. It can be bringing your family together as one and building a community that becomes a village and is better because you are a part of it. We do not know God's ways or time, Never the less, we know there is purpose in everything, your thoughts, your actions, your passions, your desire. God will receive his Glory. It is always a reason, a season, and a lifetime of lessons and experiences that you go through to become the best you,

Falling or being in love is personal. When you feel love, real love, new love it is like endorphins go off in your insides. You feel butterflies, your mind focuses on that one thing, and constant good thoughts come to mind. You feel giddy and excited. Love is like floating on cloud nine. Love is the fear of falling from the cloud, the break in the heart, the what ifs, and how will I's. Love is dangerous and yet rewarding. Love is a trust, a blind trust. You need faith with love, you need to believe with love. Love is Good Love is God, Love is that long embrace of a hug until you feel the genuine feelings from my heart, when I hold you close with a tight grip, the embrace that makes tears flow when you are vulnerable it's the trust at the moment that I am here and present and I am can be will be and represent Love.

I Love you.

What is the big dream? What is your passion that is work but doesn't seem like work because you love what you do? If money is the motivation, is it the big dream? Are your dreams limited to what you can see and feel touch? The Big Dream is the path of life that shows peace, joy and favour. Win after win. Is the big dream a house or a home, a job or a career, a car or a vehicle? The labels and words you use mean something these days. Many wealthy people pass without knowing the cause of death, a normal person without the monetary riches can provide a cause within 30 days. Interesting to see the deception of the wealthy to disguise the purpose of the reason for the loss of a life. Life is valuable and should be cherished. Live each day as it is the best day of your life. It was a statement someone shared with me that their elder shared with them. It resonates. Tomorrow is not promised. What is your dream? Did you dream big enough? Dream Big!

My dream is to release what people say about me. It is walking in who I really am.

Accepting my feelings and managing my emotions in becoming the woman God has created me to be. I denied who I loved because so many were against it. Not because he did me so terribly but because of their opinion of how he treated others. No one was in the midst of our relationship, he wanted to be my everything, my man, my friend, my strength, my encouragement and he also built me up and broke me down. Not until later did I admit if I had responded differently my life would have been different. He loved me, and he wanted to change for me but he could not trust my love, trust my loyalty due to so many negative people around with their opinions. I realize if I keep living for everyone else, I will miss my blessing and what brings me joy. I didn't want to love him, yet he taught me I am not in control of that. It is what it is.

How do you live your life fearless and bold? How to be open and honest with yourself so you can be with others. You have experienced enough life to know it is what it is. How to identify, discern the fakes, and the snakes and see the sheep with in the wolves. The bark is always out there looking for who to bite to infect with the hopeless ness of this is all it is. Things are not success, peace and joy are, there is nothing more valuable than to be able to walk in love.

Love is patient, Love is kind, love does not envy, does not boast, Love endures all.

The Bible

Dreaming Big will cost relationships with friends and family. Some people will only view you from their perspective of success. If they have not passed go and collected two hundred dollars they do not expect you to pass go and collect two hundred dollars. The Crab in a bucket mentality, don't be her or him. Be better than that. It is so amazing when you look around to see how many people actually cheer for you when you are gone and how many people hang around when you're down. When you overcome and conquer the tests and trials before you, those who you thought were real even show true colors and some of them are red, with envy and contentment because you're living your life, and not confined by their short comings or lack of motivation and dedication to create the life they desire for themselves. Life is so much more than watching TV and smoking weed. The number of people who are content complaining about other people's lives and how they live and all they are doing is watching. Talking about a dream or lack of someone else's but doing nothing to advance themselves. Change is the model. Life is no longer what it used to be, control and the enemy is on attack and we are in this world but not of this world. Don't be afraid to dream, do not allow anyone who is not for you to dictate you to be still in your life because they are still in theirs.

When I received the text I felt some kind of way. You're telling me that you need money for my brother to go to work, however, I know he is having company and not going to work. Maybe she doesn't know, but this is not something he usually hides from her. She is the type of person who pretends to go along with her husband's infidelity.

In reality, she hates it. Her fault for not standing up for her man and her feelings. The power lies in the tongue. Speak up for yourself, your dream is important. I can understand the frustration, however, taking it out on myself when I am working to build my own life back up. I have decisions to make, I need peace to see where God has purposed me to be. The enemy will attack in any way he can, and when someone has left their gate open he uses them. The situation made me angry and disappointed. It let me know what you did was not out of kindness or your heart but to use and think that you are getting over it. You take pride in thinking that you are manipulating someone, deception, and trickery are of the devil. Disappointment sets in, I thought you were real and understood my journey and come to find out, I'm not worth fighting the enemy spirit for what is right. My intent for anyone is not malicious. You can not expect you out of people and when people show you who they are, believe them. I am not there for a reason and yes, as soon as I was well I wanted to leave.

Why would that surprise anyone, I wasn't in this place before the illness and you know I don't care to be here if I can help it. When a person decides not to stay at work and make money and knows that they have rent and bills, the time off of work and the money spent at the dispensary need to be revaluated. I do not feel the least bit responsible, you leave work at will, tell me how many hours have you missed at work and have not been paid for in the last two weeks. How much is your paycheck? Is it a full paycheck, let's calculate... You said you make $20 per hour, you work 40 per week, that is $800 gross pay. Let's estimate 23% tax (very high) and it's biweekly so bring-home pay is approx $1,232 biweekly. That would be $2,832 per month. If rent is $700 and we can estimate $110 for each gas, light, water, $1,030 for household expenses.

Then add an additional $100 internet and $100 phone bill... Totals to $1,230. So if you would work your schedule and bring home your full pay you should still have $1,602 left to pay for groceries, uber and other needed items per month, pretty much $400 per paycheck if budgeted appropriately. Now if you have been dishonest about your wage and hours that is why it is not working out. If you make what you say, you have more than enough money. Play with someone else, do better. Dream Bigger.

We come into people's lives for a reason, season or a lifetime. In the between times there are lessons and blessings that we will either repeat or grow from. Change is always there. The Dream is what you are working towards the steps you take to make today better than yesterday. The reason may be for you, the Lord may use you and the reason will be for them. The Bible states A righteous person will lay down their life for their friends. Are you that friend that trusts the path set before you to walk where you can not see and may not always understand never the less trust you are on the path that was designed just for you. Standing boldly knowing no weapon formed will not prosper.

What if the challenge is just to have faith and believe without doubting? That is my husband, that is my business, that is my bank account, that is my vacation, that is my home I walk by faith and not by sight. The unseen is the dream, the reality is making it happen, walking the walk. Don't be afraid to dream big.

My family came to the north in the great migration in 1929. John Will had to have a dream that gave him the confidence to travel with his family to a land where he knew no one, where he had to lay his own foundation and raise his children. Six boys and one girl established homes, families and careers in foundry and manufacturing. The foundation was laid and the blueprint was available to follow. A dream walking by faith. Dreaming bigger than the South, dreaming of a home and having a strong family foundation. How can you create your family foundation that your children will be blessed from, the legacy of your heritage, the legacy of your history?

I said that I did not dream big enough, I achieved the things that I dreamed of and now I look at it as my God is writing the rest of my story. He has laid the plan and allowed me to achieve and now he is asking do I trust him. His Dream for me is bigger than my dream, he determines my path and my ways and I will need to trust him that he has not brought me this far to leave me, he will receive the glory from my life. I may not always be peaches and roses nevertheless I will be blessed coming and going, in the day and in the night. I can do all things through Christ who strengthens me.

Dreaming big to make this vision that God has given me come to pass. It is God's plan.

The experiences of life prepare you or equip you for the area that you are called in. For example, as a child, everyone used to play what I wanted to be, a housewife, restaurant owner or a cook, a model, an athlete, a rock star, a politician. When I was growing up, the most prestigious job was the president of the United States. As I grow older and learn more, that may just be the most stressful job there is, yet that is just my opinion. The area of your interest is also an indicator of your calling. For me it was business, I always loved business and had a natural talent for figuring out how it operates or small things that could enhance the market or encourage people to the product or service that was available. I slept on my dream and noticed my career was my education when I had the ah-ha moment of going to work in the field I enjoy. I do not like waking up each day dreading that I had to go to work in this place and I hated it.

The pay was good but I hated it. I was not growing, I was just there. That works for some people and they provide an excellent life, it was just not for me and my passion. At the time when I started the job, it was great and I loved it, I was excited and looked forward to going each day. This is a reflection on enjoying the people I am working with and enjoying the job that I am doing. This process also involves knowing what you're doing and knowing who you are.

You work to pay and cover your experiences but never stop working towards your goals and your dreams. Know what you are passionate about and you will find your path that will lead to your purpose-driven life.

Your dream is your own, if you are passionate about being a helpmate a mate will be for you. God does not make mistakes. It is learning to trust him through the unfamiliar, to know his voice and to see the lessons and the blessings of his amazing works. Everything he is above what you could imagine or think. He will provide and he will teach, he will also correct. He corrects those he loves. Be grateful for the correction; it leads you closer to a righteous life and everlasting favour.

Big Dreams will require sacrifices. You may have to let go of some things, some people and some habits. It is pressing into the uncomfortable conversations and decisions that you make that are prioritizing yourself and what you are working for, while still being kind and patient with others who may feel neglected. To achieve your dreams you have to know what you are working for and why. It may have nothing to do with the next person nor may they be supportive of you achieving your dream if they are not receiving an incentive from it. People change and people at times do not like to see change in others. Some people around you may want you to stay beneath them so they feel powerful, others may encourage you to reach the highest mountain. How will you know what your limits are if you never reach for them? Will you know how to change a chapter and start a new one? People can be categorized for a reason, a season or a lifetime. My first husband and I had children. He was in my life for a very long season but will be in my children's life for a lifetime. My second husband was in my life for a reason and only stayed a shorter season. I had a best friend, brother that came into my life for a reason and it was a long season. I will appreciate him for a lifetime, however, the season is up and love is at a distance. It has changed, my goals and priorities have changed. Sometimes you need to level up and live the life that is best for you, and not everyone is happy for you or can come. You have no bad intentions for anyone, however, when you empty out and are refilling you do not want to refill with the old wine, if so you will continue to go through the same trials and tribulations. If you want something different, if you want that dream, move differently, plan differently and follow up differently, to get different results. Dream Big!

We all were born into sin. When we were created in the womb we entered into this world of sin. By faith, we can choose the light or darkness, good or bad, hard work or free loading. There are choices that you will make that will make you a peace maker or a shit starter. No matter what it is, addressing and knowing yourself the good, the bad and the ugly will allow you to make space to make your big dream a reality. As I mentioned earlier, self-centeredness is a part of everyone's character. If you do not think about your wants and desires, how can you work towards your goals and dreams? However, where is the line from confidence to conceited? You need to know, that you need to believe in yourself but not think of yourself above others or competing with others. An honest competition to make you better such as sports events and working towards a promotion or position may be healthy competition. However, competition that causes strife, envy and jealousy is not good competition. Covetousness is not good competition, that is craving for something someone else has be it a person or things. We all have our own lane and God will make space for you if it is for you. When you begin to dabble in deception and manipulation with lies and stealing you are operating in the darkness. We all have things we need to overcome, so that time in the mirror looking at your reflection can provide insight into who you are. If you do not like your reflection, what don't you like? Address it with yourself. People can always point out the dirt in other's eyes, can you identify the dirt in your own eye? What are traits that you notice in others first, good and bad? You notice different characteristics because you are familiar with the characteristic that stands out the most to you. If you always see jealousy, you may have some jealousy in you that you will need to work out. If you see kindness, you may be a kind person who sees kindness in people. Know what is good and what is bad. The world is really black and white, humans, create the grey and try to manoeuvre our options to be right when right and wrong are instilled and a learned trait.

The fruit of the spirit is love, joy, peace, patience, kindness, goodness, faithfulness, gentleness and self-control. The acts of the flesh are sexual immorality, impurity, debauchery, Idolatry, witch craft, hatred, discord, jealousy, fits of rage, selfish ambition, dissensions, factions and envy, drunkenness, orgies and the like will not inherit the kingdom of God. These are the traits that you need to know and see as you look in the mirror. Do you have them, is your flesh controlling you or your spirit? Many of these things we can see running rampant and are popular characteristics of today. How can you begin to pluck the dirt out of your own eye so you can become and create the person and the big dream? Dream Big.

We all know that anybody can be anything if they put their mind to it and they are dedicated it can come to pass. Everyone's path is laid before them. They ask themselves what if, they ask themselves how it will be received (what people will think), but deep inside you are passionate about your idea and if it just encourages a handful you have done enough. Then you should think big, what if it encourages a community, a city, a state, a country, a nation, or a generation?? Can you trust enough to say Lord this is my dream, this is where I see me? Is this the purpose for me? Let thy will be done. Dreaming Big!

Now to execute the steps to making your dream a reality. When you look into the box from outside the box you can see the realities of what is and what is to come from the results and consequences of our choices and motives. The path that is before us is ours and ours alone and at times we have people along our paths with us. Our children and our spouses, those who are in your life at times your paths may cross and it may be for a reason a season or a lifetime, the way you manoeuvre through that relationship tells about you and your character as well as about how you think of yourself. We grow in age each year one, two three, ten eleven twelve, then the teens, the twenties, the ah-ha moment of the thirties, the rebirth in the forties and if we learned along the way the wisdom in the fifties.

Faith and Flesh

Dreaming big has much to do with how you see yourself. In finding myself I had to look within and find direction and instruction on how to manage my life. Psalms 23:1-6 states The Lord is my shepherd; I have all that I need. He lets me rest in green meadows; he leads me beside peaceful streams. He renews my strength. He guides me along the right paths, bringing honourto his name. Even when I walk through the darkest valley, I will not be afraid, for you are close beside me. Your rod and your staff protect and comfort me. You prepare a feast for me in the presence of my enemies. You honour me by anointing my head with oil. My cup overflows with blessings. Surely your goodness and unfailing love will pursue me all the days of my life, and Iwill live in the house of the Lord forever.

You can walk in faith or walk in the spirit, we acknowledge that it is mind body and spirit. We must realize the balance is being aware of all aspects of ourselves. Your faith and your flesh. Some may confuse the two or try to cloud the interpretation of what one is, by definition faith is the substance of things hoped for and the evidence of things not seen or complete trust or confidence in something or someone. The flesh would be the opposite of things that can be seen felt and touched.

Psalm 42

Why am I discouraged? Why is my heart so sad? I will put my hope in God!I will praise him again- My saviour and my God!

What a beautiful day. To start off with a distraction to lead you to be obedient to the word. To release and have reason to release. My praise is mine and personal and I will walk in truth to who I am in love with My Lord and Savior Jesus Christ. He has got me! He is so good and I love talking about Him! Let me teach you in the name of

33

Jesus. Lord lay the path you have set before me. I trust you, Jesus. YOu equip the called. You will be told to each and every person.We will believe it again! Salvation is upon us! Let the church say AMEN!!

The fact that all of these people witnessed the chaos that surrounded my life and now see the transformation of cleansing and being filled with new wine. It is the journey. It's not what you go through but how you go through it. He has made a way out of no way, transitioned, trafficked, tolerated and took over! For this I am grateful.

When the Lord lifts His countenance upon us, it shows that He is looking at us for our good. God wants to bless us. He wants to protect us. He wants to make His face shine upon us, be gracious to us and give us peace. Here is the Blessing, the most obvious meaning of thisphrase is that God accepts us.

The Psalm writer states that God is the health of their countenance, meaning that He is the source of their joy, peace, patience, etc. Psalm 42:11;

Psalm 43:5

Why art thou cast down, O my soul? And why art thou disquieted within me? Hope in God: ForI shall yet praise him, Who is the health of my <u>countenance</u>, and my God.

Discipline

Walking uprightly and boldly is required to Dream Big. You must believe in your dreams to work and make them a reality. You need to be bold because there will always be someone on your shoulder trying to convince you to give up. Thus dusting your shoulders off becomes a frequent activity when God gives you a vision to pursue especially when it leans to your purpose. There will be obstacles and the test is how you handle the obstacles or giants, mountains that are set before you, it is how you deal with them that produces your character thus making your Big Dream a reality.

There will be people who walk out of your life that you can clearly see the enemy work through. Loving them though, distancing yourself if need be, and trusting the direction of your life. Will you stay committed when it does not look like you want it or you get a no when you want a yes? Will you stay focused when everything falls apart and you need to start over? It is not what you go through but how you go through it.

When a flashlight grows dim or quits working, you don't throw it away, you change the batteries.

When a person messes up and finds themselves in a dark place, Do you cast them aside? Of course not,

You help them change their batteries!

Some need AA ... Attention and Affection;Some need AAA

Attention, affection, and acceptance;Some need C..

Compassion; Some need D..

Direction

And if they still don't seem to shine...

Simply sit with them quietly and share your light.

In becoming purposeful, know how to share your light and how. It is a dark world and those with the light... It is ok to shine. Dream Big.

When the big idea begins to develop it may not all happen at once. I know the dream placed on my heart has been in the making for years. As I think back as I grew in character my dream grew with me. My eyes were opened to experiences and opportunities that I would have never had if I had not stepped out on faith and pursued my passions. Your passion and your gift will make room for you. How you make money or how you spend your day can be filled and fulfilling if you just trust yourself and your gifts. You need to stand strong and work towards that dream, that life, that hobby that soothes your soul. It's peaceful and full of joy and if you walk infaith and trust God's direction you will know and be able to identify when the opps or the enemy is attacking. How you deal with it, showing a better way there is nothing stronger than love.

You have power in being you. Nobody else can be you, you were created to be great! Being great is not always fame or fortune, my greatness is joy, peace and love. The rest will come, no matter what state you're in to learn to be content and faithful, blessings will come if those blessing=-08=7-09 are meant for you. God has enough room for all of us, and if there is no room He makes room. That is how awesome he really is! Dream Big.

What are the dreams that you have on the inside? The dream no one can see the true honesty between you and your soul. Your inner being of your true authentic self. Yourself without regret, jealousy, or envy. Yourself without anyone else involved, that reflection of just you. Not your past hurts or traumas, not your wins or losses. It is yours. Your desires of your heart, your knowledge and experiences, your choices and consequences the lessons and the blessings that make up authentically you.

I want to be a wife. I want to be a helpmate to my husband, I want to allow him to lead and support and encourage him, I want to have a voice and feel loved and appreciated. I want to live our life without anyone else, we parent our kids and guide our grandkids. Show love and support but encourage success and leadership. We will pray together, we are a force alone, we are Blessed together, and we will give God the glory each and every day that will show in our love and compassion for one another, our smile and contentment where God has us. We will have a home, a home for us and our family. A family home, with a yard, garage, multiple bathrooms and bedroom for the grandkids, one for the girls and one for the boys.

I want to love deeply. I want to love more than the flesh. I want to care how you feel in the morning, I want to be your peace at night. I want to feel stronger when we are together and stronger when we are apart. I want us to have each other like we have ourselves, we are one. What is mine is his, what is his is mine, we want the best for each other and support each other's goals and visions. We enjoy yet waste not, the Lord will bless us when we come and when we go, He goes before us because he loves us and we are His own. He did not bring us this far to leave us. He did not connect us this way for no reason. He has a purpose in all, we have to believe. We have to trust, We have to Dream Big.

Did I mention Dreaming Big will cost you? To grow beyond who you were and beyond others who are around you will cost you. It will cost you friendships, family and relationships. Some people only want you big enough for them to step over you, some want you to remain beneath them, in sin so they feel better about themselves. Growth and Big Dreams will show you the true character of those you are associated with. You knew that person did not clap for you in the small wins, what did you expect when you win Big? You begin to see once you step outside and look in. You support a stranger but will not support your cousin or friend. You click like on strangers and people that do not care for you yet you will look over the childhood friend that finally had their dreams come true.

37

People support each other in their darkness more than they do in the light. Is it because they are afraid that other people will shine too brightly? Do you not realize that it is a Godly light and itshines on you too? There needs to be more encouragement in the light. People will have trauma bond, and enemy bond, collaborating together to gang up on one person and feel accomplished not seeing that they are just being a bully and their negative opinion tells more about them than it does about the person attempting to build their life among all of this darkness. So many people walk daily in the sacrifice for others and then when they feel weak, only to look around and see all those who supported them be now here found. Progress is a lonely road, in actually as the fake falls off, you were already on this road, just distracted by the illusion that they   really loved you. Love does not envy, does not boast, is not jealous, and does not covet or think of itself more than it should. It is kind and patient, Love endures.

The dream is big, and it is bigger than you think. It is God's purpose and God's plan He is trusting you to Manage and Grow the Dream Accordingly. We have to trust Him, though Jesus we are saved and He has ordered our steps. Walking where you can't see is scary, Walking in Faith knowing God ordered your steps. See the supernatural in the natural. In Jesus's name, we always pray, that is the way to the kingdom of Heaven. Dreams can be the Visions and Destiny that were planned for you before you were born. Dream Big, it's your destiny.

As you mature the Big Dreams go beyond the material things. Yes I want the big house yet my focus is a home, I want a home. Yes, I would like that Camery of my dreams yet I am grateful just for transportation. I long for a marriage, I will not settle for the team. This commitment may leave you lonely, seeking attention, and longing for connection. This is when you really have to trust that God will do what he said he would do. I question whether is this my desire or your direction. One real friend is better than many friends with agendas.

Your circle and your circle's circle are the influence of your attitude and many times your altitude. There is always someone in the group who has achieved more or aspires to be more. Is the circle clapping or breaking off into smaller clicks and bonding over the negative talk of one of the circles? Not until I stepped out of the circle and then looked back in did I realize that I was in the centre alone and everyone bonded over the negative feelings towards me. And then there was silence. To dream big you have to be in tune with you, in tune with your dream. When you're working on your dream many distractions will come. The first ones will be the obvious and then you grow past them. Soon you will need to become aware of your surroundings. What is taking your attention? Life is short so balance is good, change is necessary. You need to work toward your dream.

I feel like I have been working on this dream forever. As I matured the dream matured. I look and I can see the development from one stage to another. I had to grow within those stages to be prepared for the journey my life was set on. The heartaches are lessons and the relationships are blessings. Through them all being consistent and staying focused is important. It's bigger than me

It's bigger than You

It's not bigger than Us!

Working together is important. My owner is my God through Jesus Christ. He allows me to manage his vision through me. In this role of management is responsibility the more given the more the responsibility. Not to talk the talk but walk the walk. This will not be an easy journey, however, all things work together for my good. Worldwide beyond any of my expectations, changing lives, encouraging the light, standing strong like a tree planted. Dream Big!

Self Esteem is defined as:

Self-esteem is how we value and perceive ourselves. It's based on our opinions and beliefs about ourselves, which can feel difficult to change. We might also think of this as self-confidence.

In this journey of Dreaming Big self-discovery is important. This big Dream is yours and about you in order to make it a reality you need to know yourself, know your dream and believe in yourself enough to know if God gave you the vision he will give you the provision to make it a reality, The road may not be easy and there will be some battles, Nevertheless in the end you know the kingdom of the one true God thru Jesus wins. How do you prepare for the battle? How do youstrengthen yourself in the storm? You have to believe in yourself, your self-esteem, and your self-confidence and trust God he has a purpose in all that he does. Do you trust Him? Do you believe in Him?

At times my soul screams OH GOD this hurts, what am I to get out of this? Am I going through this correctly, is it even about me? I am valuable and I can be used by God.

There are 3 ranges of self-esteem:

- Overly high self-esteem: Feeling superior to others. People with overly high self-esteemare often arrogant, self-indulgent, and express feelings of entitlement. ...

- Low self-esteem: Feeling inferior to others. ...

- Healthy self-esteem: Having an accurate and balanced self-view. How to boost self-esteem?

Be kind to yourself

- Get to know yourself. For example, what makes you happy and what you value in life. ...

- Try to challenge unkind thoughts about yourself. ...

- Say positive things to yourself. ...

- Practice saying no. ...

- Try to avoid comparing yourself to others. ...

- Do something nice for yourself.

What are the 7 steps to improve your self-esteem?

By: Judy Zellner, LPCC

- Stop comparing yourself to others. ...

- Stop belittling yourself. ...

- Use positive self-affirmations to build our self-esteem. ...

- Surround yourself with positive, supportive people. ...

- Dwell on your positive qualities. ...

- Give back. ...

- Pay attention to self-care.

How do you fix low self-esteem?

Here are some other simple techniques that may help you feel better about yourself.

- Recognise what you're good at. We're all good at something, whether it's cooking,singing, doing puzzles or being a friend. ...

- Build positive relationships. ...

- Be kind to yourself. ...

- Learn to be assertive. ...

- Start saying "no" ...

- Give yourself a challenge.

What are the 5 C's of self-esteem?

The 5Cs are Competence, Confidence, Character, Connection, and Caring [1]. Confidence reflects a positive sense of self-worth, mastery, future, positive identity and self-efficacy.

Competence is a view of one's capabilities with respect to a given domain or vocation.

What causes low self-esteem?Causes of low self-esteem

Unhappy childhood where parents (or other significant people such as teachers) were extremely critical. Poor academic performance in school results in a lack of confidence. Ongoing stressful life events such as relationship breakdown or financial trouble.

What are the signs of low self-esteem?

Signs of low self-esteem include:

- saying negative things and being critical about yourself.

- joking about yourself in a negative way.

- focusing on your negatives and ignoring your achievements.

- blaming yourself when things go wrong.

- thinking other people are better than you.

- thinking you don't deserve to have fun.

What are the signs of low confidence?

Signs of low confidence may include:

- feelings of self-doubt.

- passive or submissive behaviour.

- difficulty trusting others.

- feeling inferior to others.

- overly sensitive to criticism.

- feeling unloved.

How do I love myself?

How to Love Yourself: Ways to Start Loving Yourself Again

- Let go of all your regrets and past mistakes. ...

- Don't compare yourself to others. ...

- Do things that make you happy. ...

- Embrace contentment. ...

- Increase positive emotions. ...

- Surround yourself with positive people. ...

- Practice loving-kindness meditation. ...

- Set boundaries.

Can you develop low self-esteem?

Low self-esteem often begins during childhood and results from hearing or interpreting messages from significant people including parents, siblings, friends and teachers, who were often very critical.

How can I be confident and love myself?

Surround Yourself With Positivity Seek out relationships that make you feel good about yourself and avoid those that bring you down or make you feel negative. Similarly, try to fill your social media feeds and daily input with positive messages, quotes, and affirmations that remind you of your worth and potential.

What are the six rules of self-esteem?

The six pillars of self-esteem are:

- Living consciously. ...

- Accepting oneself. ...

- Taking responsibility for oneself's actions. ...

- Being self-assertive. ...

- Living with a purpose. ...

- Having personal integrity.

How do I help my partner with low self-esteem?

Here are some suggestions on how to talk to them, to try to support them:

- Remain autonomous. First of all, accept that you are not there to 'fix' your partner. ...

- Avoid flippant compliments. ...

- Help them to see a new perspective. ...

- Encourage practising self-love. ...

- Don't walk on eggshells.

Having Big Dreams and the pursuit of those dreams can find yourself in reality all by yourself. As I look around and assess. There were times when I had many people around me, always something to do the life of the party, and fun had for all who were around. I drink you drink, I smoke you smoke, I have a new outfit you get a new outfit. He treats me, he treats you... Where are those people, oh they left when I left the streets or grew up a little bit. Then it was college and family meeting new people new experiences new things, we helped and supported each other, encouraged yet it was the 90s so still fun. Then you grow up, and get married, where did everyone go? Marriage goes bad, where are you now? Oh, a new life still trying but the juice is still sour. Stand up Get up stay focused, you can do this don't give up. Grow up, press through. Life happens the winds blow and the times change run home where it is safe, and run home where you can rest. Family call you home only to criticise and remind you why you left in the first place. Looking at the Bid Dream I was always alone. No matter who you try to include or to save or share, It is your dream and yours alone. Where are the people who believe in you, it's those who don't have access to your vulnerabilities, it's those who do not know your faults or have been swayed by a group of your close friends and family. Those people are usually the stranger you meet who knows you at who you are now. Your plea for those who have watched you would like to see your growth and your success through the pain. Yet all they do is lash out and mention your faults, Yes! It is ok, I know my dream I know my passion and I am getting to know my strength.

Your strength to endure all of the attacks from the enemy that try to slow your progress to your purpose. Your strength to grow in the storm and swim even if it is the doggy paddle. You know how to push and pull, you know where your help comes from. I find gratitude a two-way street, I am grateful for all those who stood with me in life and assisted in any way even if it was a smile. I may have needed it that day. I also think gratitude is covered for those who are blessed in order to bless others. I am grateful that I am blessed to be a blessing in any circumstance. All things are Gods, my Gods. It's seeing the love in the small things that will get you into Heaven. Some people do not dream of going there, some will settle for hell. I have learned in the Big Dream we all have free will and the Lord will give you the desires of your heart, but at what cost? Is it your desire that you are seeking because you see potential or is it the walk of faith that God has you on to save someone else, to build you so you can endure the next level of life that your Dream develops in? Tests and trials will come, how do you show love? How do you respond? I can not control what you do, I can control how I respond. I trust Jesus, I know he did not bring me this far to leave me. Teach me to Respond, God has a plan and a purpose for me so I must continue to Dream Big!

We all need to take time and evaluate our lives. Are you living or existing? Do your days run together with no excitement or change? Is your routine, income pattern the exact same as last year? Change comes as an obstacle to some, many people do not like change. Allow me to ask, how is there growth without change? A seed is planted and then it sprouts roots, roots grab a hold of the dirt and become strong to form a foundation to bloom. In that process, it is steps that change and grow into the desired result, bloom. Are you existing or living? Are you living or just existing? Are you settling for the comfortable or are you willing to press through thetough times to receive the desired results?

15 signs that you are just existing instead of living. How do they apply to your life?

1. Little Physical Activity

a. Are you walking, or going outside to move your muscles

b. Do you have a stretch routine

2. Procrastination and Laziness

a. What do you do all day

b. Does your day produce results

3. Neglecting Responsibilities

a. Are your bills paid on time

b. Have you spoken to and/or encouraged your children, partner, parents

4. Frequent Escapism

a. Do you daydream

b. Do you wish you were somewhere else doing something different

5. Feeling empty or Depressed

a. How do you feel inside

b. Do you have joy

6. Lack of Meaningful Relationships

a. Who do you talk to daily/weekly when you are up/down or all around

b. Who do you tell and feel that you love them/ Who tells you

c. Who do you value/ do they value you

7. Constant Boredom

a. Do you say I'm bored, post it on social media

b. Do you have something to fill your time at all times

8. Excessive Time Spent on Screens

a. How long do you spend on social media platforms

9. Neglecting Personal Hygiene

a. When was the last time you cleaned your body, hair teeth

b. Is your clothes clean

10. No Goals or Ambitions

a. Today is like yesterday

b. Nothing is changing for tomorrow

c. Are you okay with that

11. Time Passes Quickly

a. Are your days flying by without important moments or experiences

12. Negative Self Talk

a. How do you speak to yourself

b. Do you love you

13. Boring Routine

a. What is your daily pattern?

b. Is there joy and laughter

14. Avoiding Social Interactions

a. Do you stay away just not to talk to people

b. Do you show a poor attitude/ Is your face turned up / resting bitch face so no onespeaks to you?

15. No Hobbies or Interests

a. Do you do anything that you enjoy that brings you peace happiness or a sense ofaccomplishment?

Learn your Life, Live your life. No longer exist but be purposeful in your intent every day. Add a walk to your routine or a song to your morning. Make up your bed or clean the kitchen before relaxing for the night. Your life is what you make of it, your day is the moments you capture and make count. Your passion is the gift from within that brings you joy, peace and happiness. Not every day will be easy, nevertheless, when there is a will there's a way to introduce change and growth into your life so you are no longer existing but living the life that you desire and deserve. Dream Big and make your dream a reality. It is time.

The dreams that you have are a God-given vision for the blessings and purpose that he has designed for your life. God knew Eve was going to offer the Apple, he knew Adam would be weak. God designed us just as we are and he allowed us to have a choice in life, he provides guidance and expectations to live by in order to participate in His kingdom. The enemy will mess with your mind and make you believe it is about control, once you know Jesus for yourself and begin to seek His kingdom for yourself you will begin to learn that what he does and will always continue to do is out of love. In order to be present in his kingdom you will need to walk in love with all people at all times. We are imperfect people and God knows that he created us this way so we can openly seek him and welcome him into our lives. As the enemy inclines your ear to manipulate you into sin, and for you to think sin is good and love is weak. In my weakness He, my God, my Lord Jesus is strong. So if I am weak to love you are confused because that is when He is strong. I am stronger than I have ever been in my weakness. My Father has my back. Through the Christ in me, I can carry on, Dream Big and watch his wonders work through my life. When we stand at the old rugged cross, I seek the Lord and hope he says"Child well done." You have the Holy Spirit, you walk in the Holy Spirit, I see me (Jesus) in you. In Heaven, there is no confusion, or chaos, no backstabbing or gossip, no murder or death. It is life and life more abundantly. Don't be misled or tricked, the play of the enemy has not changed, He has taken the requirements to enter into Heaven and into God's peace and made a mockery. Those who do not have a personal relationship with God can be led astray and think they are seeking and praying to the saviour and the whole time digging further away down the rabbit hole where the enemy encourages them to think that they can not be saved from their sin. The Devil is a Lie! You, Us, We can all be saved by the Grace of God! Seek him out and find out. Everyone's journey and path has been designed for them, your choices as you travel down the road will produce consequences and results... How you live determines the path of life. Dream Big, keep it simple and keep working towards the goal of salvation. It's not about the material things.

When I think about my dream. It is to be a wife and establish a strong family. That is truly what I desire. A Husband that protects and provides and is an example of strength and wisdom for my children and children's children establishing a family foundation for generations to come. It is not all about the right here and now enjoy the moments and build the foundations.

In pursuit of the Big Dream, we have to take the time to listen for direction from the Lord. I need to build a foundation that my children can stand on. A foundation of stability, financial and physical, a foundation of faith, truth and honesty. Build a foundation of Faith and know that our Help comes from the Lord. A testimony that states I put it all in Jesus's hands. He interceded on my behalf. He goes to his father and mediates for me. He paid for my sins and sent the Holy Spirit to guide and lead me. You are reading this now, I live my best life, full of peace, full of joy. Waiting for the time to walk the streets of gold in Heaven. Setting

up your treasures in Heaven. Not now not here not to impress mere men. My treasure is in Heaven, that is where my mansion is, that is where the streets are paved in gold. Not a yellow brick road that leads to destruction, not blindly walking into what I know is not pleasing to my father to my helper to my saviour. I am setting my treasures in Heaven working on me until the day of Jesus' return. I want to be called and chosen. I want to be faithful and loyal, I want God to be well pleased knowing that it is He that is in me that is greater than this world. I am in this place but not of this place. If God is for me He is more than the World against me. Thank you Jesus for the Big Dream.

In the obstacles of life, you can discover your purpose and begin a plan for your journey. The obstacles teach you how to be strong and how to deal with a situation. The results may vary, however, if you continue to grow and learn at some point that obstacle will be an obstacle no more.

You will have figured out how to overcome that obstacle to where it can and will no longer hinder you from the path or goal you are working for. It's not what you go through but how you go through it. Yes, it is tough and sometimes hard, however, if you keep your mind positive and focused on the goal it will lead you to a more peaceful process. Keep Focused, Keep the Faith.

I often wonder why I do the things that I do, we were taught to not ask why, However when it comes to myself I need to understand my intentions of why I am doing a thing. Am I learning my lesson, is this a blessing, is this bringing me closer to the life or dream that I desire for myself?

How do I get closer to becoming a wife, and building a strong foundation for my family? How do I develop that business idea, what are the steps that I take? Is this relationship beneficial to the expected end? Does this person even have the capacity to support you in your dreams and visions? I am the righteousness of God and I can do all things through Christ that strengthens me. I am in this world but not of this world, God gave me a

dream of how I can be purposeful in giving Him Glory for all that he has done for me. I am going to go get that Life I dreamed of. A place here a place there a place so I can go anywhere. This is my dream, my life, I am that boss, I am that leader, I am that manager, I am that mom, I am that NaNa, I am that Child of God. I am Her. This is my dream. My Big Dream.

What does the woman represent in the Bible?

The Hebrew Bible often portrays women as victors, leaders, and heroines with qualities Israel should emulate. Women such as Hagar, Tamar, Miriam, Rahab, Deborah, Esther, and Yael/Jael, are among many female "saviours" of Israel.

(What is the real name of the Samaritan woman?)

Photini aka

Photini aka the Samaritan woman at the well

This is the name the Eastern Orthodox church has given to the Samaritan woman at the well in John 4. The story of Photini is one of the longest stories in the Bible about a woman and **it is the longest conversation that Jesus is recorded as having with anyone.**

Did the woman at the well follow Jesus?

Throughout this conversation she demonstrates a posture of discipleship, learning from Jesus, and now she is called an **evangelist**. She leaves her water jar behind—just as the disciples left their fishing nets—*a sign of her complete embrace of this calling to followJesus.*

Why did Jesus talk to the Samaritan woman at the well?

The story of the Samaritan woman, also known as the woman at the well, draws our attention to the central themes of the Gospel. By approaching her, **Jesus demonstrates His care for all, regardless of their social standing.** We can also be inspired by the Samaritan woman's excitement in sharing the good news of Jesus.

What did the woman at the well do in the Bible?

John 4:5-30

Jacob's well was there, and so Jesus, wearied as he was with his journey, sat down beside the well. It was about the sixth hour. There came a woman of Samaria to draw water.

Jesus said to her, "Give me a drink." For his disciples had gone away into the city to buy food.

What does a well mean spiritually?

Jesus used the well water as an <u>analogy</u> to represent God's fountain of life, given through Jesus for our salvation. The scenario between Jesus and the woman continued with her asking Jesus for the water of eternal life, literally thinking she would never have to return to Jacob's well at all.

Why was the Samaritan woman drawing water at noon?

Fear had a way of making this Samaritan woman do a crazy thing. She went to the well at noon, in the worst part of the day to be outside. But she goes there at that time precisely because she knows that no one will be there then.

Was the woman at the well immoral?

One commentary refers to her as "this immoral woman of Samaria."1 The author notes that the woman had been married to and divorced from five husbands. Not only that—this commentary says she was presently committing adultery with a sixth man who was not her husband.

What happened to the woman at the well after?

Her continuing witness is said to have brought so many to the Christian faith that she is described as "equal to the apostles". Eventually, having drawn the attention of Emperor Nero, she was brought before him to answer for her faith, suffering many tortures and dying a martyr after being thrown down a dry well.

Did Jesus tell the woman at the well to go and sin no more?

[11] She said, No man, Lord. And Jesus said unto her, Neither do I condemn thee: go andsin no more. [12] Then spake Jesus again unto them, saying, I am the light of the world: **he that followeth me shall not walk in darkness, but shall have the light of life.**

What sin did the woman at the well commit?

Adultery

Not only that—this commentary says she was presently committing adultery with a sixth man who was not her husband. Most commentators, preachers, and Bible teachers paint a similar portrait of the Samaritan woman Jesus speaks with in John 4. They would have us think she's a conniving adultress shunned by her community.

Who did the woman at the well become?

The Samaritan woman whom Jesus meets at Jacob's Well gleans much from her long conversation with Jesus. When she discovers his identity as the Messiah she leaves her water jar, much like the disciples left their nets, and becomes an effective evangelist to her community.

How did Jesus connect with the woman at the well?

As He was resting, a woman of the town came to fetch water, and He asked her for a drink. She was surprised at His request, for Jews did not associate with Samaritans. Jesus responded that if she knew who she was talking to, she would have asked Him for a drink.

Why did the woman at the well leave behind her jar?

The woman was so eager to bear witness to Jesus that she even left her water jar behind (v. 28). Ordinarily, women in that culture would not leave such things at the well, but this woman could not wait to tell others about Christ and would not even pause for a second to retrieve her possession.

What does the woman at the well symbolize?

Representing the lowest of the low – a female in a society where women are both demeaned and disregarded, a race traditionally despised by Jews, and living in shame as a social outcast – **she not only has a holy encounter with Christ but also receives eternal salvation.**

What is significant about the woman at the well?

The passage reveals the Samaritan woman as an astute **person who wanted to know the truth about worshipping God.** Rather than being a social outcast, she seeks out the people in her village to tell them about Jesus. They obviously respected her and went with her to learn more about Jesus.

What lessons can we learn from the woman at the well?

If we go to school to the Samaritan woman at the well, what lessons can we learn for women in the church today? There are at least three dimensions to the instruction to be received from this unnamed woman, having to do with daring to question, with openness to truth and with taking responsibility.

What is the meaning of Jesus and the woman at the well?

The story of the woman at the well demonstrates that Jesus comes to the least of these. He cares for the outcasts of society. The Samaritan woman was considered inferior because of her sex, ethnicity, and relationship history, but none of that mattered to Jesus because he saw her need for salvation.

John 4 NIV

Jacob's well was there, and Jesus, tired as he was from the journey, sat down by the well. It was about noon. 7 When a Samaritan woman came to draw water ...

The Woman at the Well · John 5 · Listen · John 6:35

I am ready to heal.

Healing is a process where we are wounded and it scabs over. Many will fall and open up the wound over and over. Some wounds are deep, some are just scratches. Some wounds can be like surgery and wounds from the inside, where it's torn and stretched yet the surface looks clean and smooth. Behaviors and thought patterns can be wounds that need to be healed. The changing of your mind, the upgrading of your thoughts, and the seeking of knowledge to make you better are ways to heal the inside. How do you heal the spirit? The flesh takes time to heal, you have to clean the wound, you have to cover it and expose it to air and water. You will need to allow it to scab over, to regrow the skin. Some grow thicker. Is this how the spirit heals? Do you forgive, to be forgiven, forgive them, forgive you? Do you pray for guidance, seek ye the kingdom of God. Do you rest in peace, take time to quiet all of the noise around you so you can hear yourself, look at yourself in the mirror and see what the eyes reflect? What brings you peace? Do you have a plan, a direction, a goal, or something that you are working towards? Personal, Business, Hobby, what makes you happy? Do you know, do you feel, are you angry? How do you heal?

Stand on Business, the business of you. I am who I say I am. You say I am dumb, I say totalk to you, You say I'm childish, I say nope I don't want to be a part of your group of friends. My words, I am the only one of your girls strong enough to walk away. You talk to me like I am the last, the last shall be first. Don't fumble with me. I am valuable and Jesus loves me. I believe what he told me, I believe that I am meant for more and that He is preparing me for himself, to be of value to His Kingdom.

He is giving me the confidence and the strength to walk the journey he has prepared for me before I was born. My mom knows there is something special about me, yet she treats me so, that my family sees the favour of God on me and shows their jealous or envious head. I don't have friends because of the favour God has on my life and the lack of tolerance of BS when it comes to me and my time. I seek the light of the Lord and the people of God can see the glow. I give all glory to God for saving me, for choosing me. That Guy sees the glory in me and he deals with envy and jealous tendencies. The Lord God, my Jesus will prepare a table in the presence of my enemies, the journey may be long and lonely with God I can do all things. I am grateful and appreciate His blessings and the lessons that I learned along the way.

The guy tries to put me down and feel less, why because you know that I am the righteousness of God. I am blessed and I am going to walk in it. Thank you, Jesus. You are my everything and if God is for me, he is more than the world against me. I know he loves me and is fighting the enemy with a narcissistic attitude that will break you in the end. He will be broken and I pray the Lord strengthens him and rebuilds him the way it needs to be. As for myself, yes I could have lost my life, but the Lord saw purpose in me for another day, He sent me back for you, are you coming? I Got things to do.

There will be times when you will not be working on the goal, but you will be in the meantime learning and gaining the strength to endure the next level of what is coming next. I will dress for success and I will focus on work and balancing my life to win. My first financial goal then on to setting goals for business and development. I am asking the Lord to lead me in his way and have his will be done in my life. The life that I now live I live for Christ. I didn't have the desire to go on at one point in time and then the Lord said trust me. I got you. He can fuss and have girls, childish I am not. You are my husband, however you will learn to respect me and protect me at all costs. Your conversation will be that it is not worth losing her, if you don't feel this way about me we don't need to be together. Twenty years with the same girl, and I am stupid, I don't get it. You have plenty and they just accept you to do whatever it is that you do and they are happy that you took the time to be with them not complaining or holding to you any expectation. Who does that? The fact that you do not spend on them like you do me? What is wrong? Dude I am your wife, you will learn to grow and respect me. You can choose the light but me sitting and being a yes person while you fall into hell will not work for me. Those dummies ruined you, they are the dummies. Unappreciative, you are the one who does not know a blessing when they see it. You wish you were me. You know I am who you love, your disrespect is too disrespectful.

I don't care if you don't call me. Then I don't have to worry about anyone calling to makeI feel like shit.

That mental abuse shit doesn't work on me. I evolve, I'm a childish boy, please. I am childish because I am unable to express myself because you are not even on my level and I must dumb myself down to speak to you I sound childish because I am dumbing myself down which makes you feel like I'm beneath you. Stop it!

Jesus Loves Me. Stop talking to me like me Jesus don't be rocking. He was with me in the fire, through the storm, in the cold lonely nights and the dark moments. My help comes from the Lord, not man. You did what you did, I did not ask you for anything or give you the impression that I was pressed about anything. You don't know my dreams goals or desires. We have nothing to talk about. I talk about God, my babies, and my job, I want to grow and talk about business and building a strong family with love. I want to celebrate wins and encourage people; I want to be strong-minded and focused to be the best I can be. God did not bring me this far to leave me and you are crazy if you think I will let the enemy in you stop me. I have made it this far by the grace of my God and I will continue to trust in His Grace. Giving God, and Jesus glory every step of the way. I am so done with this game of light and dark the world is playing. I am team Jesus and I want to prepare for battle each and every day. Let's talk about Him, let's learn about Him, Who is He, the Holy Spirit and God. Knowledge is power.

I tell you what, I will be your friend and here for you because loneliness is going to hit you like a ton of bricks. Your character is going to have to learn some hard lessons if you do not begin to repent. You may know but the enemy has a hold of you, you need to get that up off of you. I pray Lord Jesus helps us heal, helps us grow, and helps us to do your will. In Jesus name, I pray.

This is a new season, it feels like levelling up. Being more wiser and aware of your surroundings, you see the messages that are provided and you know your Father's voice. The inner knows to run concerns andteaches you to discern between good and evil. Once you see the warnings and then the action shows confirmation of the message. If there is chaos or/and confusion it is not of God. Not my God. It is a lesson or a blessing and you will continue to go through the lesson until you realize and learn and see the blessing, and it could not even be for you. First comes the Natural then the Super natural. An easy way to explain this is that you're attracted to a person, naturally and you sleep with a person, naturally, then a sperm leaves a male's body and enters into a female's womb and then merges into one to create an embryo. The embryo then grows into an egg that incubates into a baby that then grows with in a woman for some time and then is born into what we call a baby.

The supernatural occurs when you take the electrons and neutrons to create the powers within that develop the characteristics. The supernatural aspects of family, family are what we call genes. The brown hair or brown eyes, the light skin or the bronze tone, the bowed legs or big bones. The traits that are similar along a family line. Can they all sing, are they all smart? Do they all work or do they all gossip? Do they all lie, do they all live here or there? What makes them the same? What makes them different? The supernatural are the things you can not see, are they a forward thinker or more of an addicted nature? Things you can see from the bloodline, the family, the relatives.

The supernatural of thought? What is your favourite color? Is it red, or is it green? Why is it your favourite color? As I think about this question I would answer in red. Red is my favourite color. It is because I think of the blood of Jesus and am reminded to place his blood in my heart and above my door. That is me.

The point of red is a very popular favourite color and can be for many reasons. In one season of my life I found myself trying to pick any color but red because everyone else liked red. I did not want to be a follower or like something just because I was influenced by the popular opinion at that time. In this thought, I gained strength knowing that tho a popular opinion, I have my own opinion and reasoning for my own opinion for MY life. That is the only time MY opinion really matters. Even in that, not my will but yours (MY Jesus) be done.

The supernatural of the soul. What is the soul? The meaning of Soul is the immaterial essence, animating principle, or acuating cause of an individual life. As you go through life, the opinions of others often change how you view yourself and you can easily lose your way by listening to the voice of others, often words of disapproval and feelings of worthlessness. According to Plato, the three parts of the soul are the rational, spirited and appetitive parts. The Bible teaches that we consist of body, soul and spirit: "May your whole spirit, soul and body be preserved blameless at the coming of our Lord Jesus" (I Thessalonians 5:23). Our material bodies are evident, but our souls and spirits are less distinguishable. In many religious and philosophical traditions, the soul is the spiritual essence of a person, which includes one's identity, personality, and memories, an immaterial aspect or essence of a living being that is believed to be able to survive physical death.

Do all souls belong to God?

Ezekiel 18:4 King James Version (KJV)

Behold, <u>all souls are mine</u>; as the soul of the father, so also the soul of the son is mine: the soul that sinneth, it shall die.

Where does the soul go after death?

Heaven and Hell

In Christian theology St. Augustine spoke of the soul as a "rider" on the body, making clear the split between the material and the immaterial, with the soul representing the "true" person. However, although the body and soul were separate, it was not possible to conceive of a soul without its body.

The heart is thought of as the seat of the soul, hence, metaphorically, a synonym for soul.

Your spirit is the part of you that is not physical and that consists of your character and feelings. The human spirit is virtually indestructible. The soul is the seat of personality; man's will, intellect, and emotion all lie in the soul. The spirit is the part with which man communicates with the spiritual realm. The body is the part with which man communicates with the physical realm. The soul is in the middle of these two parts.

It seems that 1 Thessalonians 5:23 means "all of us." When Paul prays, "May your whole spirit and soul and body be kept blameless," he means, "your whole being." This is like Jesus telling us to "love the Lord your God with all your heart and with all your soul and with all your strength and with all your mind"

When we die, we are with Him. And we keep being with Him after our bodily resurrection and the world is made new. However, when someone dies apart from Jesus, they enter eternity carrying the weight of their offences against an infinite and holy God and are judged accordingly by Him.

Who holds our souls in life?

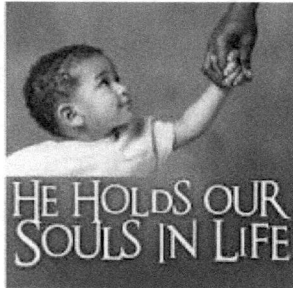

Psalm 66:8-9. The praise of God holds your soul in life.

The soul who sins is the one who will die. The son will not share the guilt of the father, nor will the father share the guilt of the son. The righteousness of the righteous man will be credited to him, and the wickedness of the wicked will be charged against him.

Soul cravings are about our needs, self-care, self-respect, self-awareness, boundaries, mental health, physical health, emotional health, and soul health. Some cravings, however, can be more destructive. A big and important part of our life is about managing our soul cravings. Purpose - flitting through life is fun, but our souls thrive on finding meaning and purpose in what we do. Contributing to others is vital to our soul's growth. Peace - finding peace through faith, mindfulness, music, through connecting to a deeper and higher order enriches our souls.

This man is everything I want in a man. The mystery and intrigue, the respect and fear, the man I would desire to be my head if I lived the other life inside of me. God you brought him near, you brought him to me. To give up everything and follow him?? No SiR! God did not bring me this far to leave me. If you are real and on that side OH how great is the man My Jesus has for me? If that is real, this has to be real, this I have to believe in. I must know that the thoughts you have placed in me are real and can and will come to frustration. God, you are mighty in all of your ways and can do all things but fail. Show me your ways oh Lord, show me your vision. This dream was placed in me many years ago and has developed me every step of the way. Obstacles will come and I am identifying my Giants. Thank you for the rocks, the rocks of your word and direction, the slowing of my pace so I can see your work. The small hints and the test of whether am I listening. It's bigger than me, It's bigger than you, It's not bigger than the US! I can do all things through Christ that Strengthens me. No, I won't go meet the devil knowing it's the devil because the devil does not bless his people. He only comes to seek to kill and destroy. Mind, body and soul belong to Jesus and if you are not a man of MY Jesus, you could never lead me. I value my loyalty and integrity. I love you, I love everyone. My God is love and I walk in Him.

The dream becomes bigger than a source of income. The dream is bigger than me, the dream is bigger than you, and the dream is not bigger than us. We must prepare and be sure to work towards our

67

goals, the dreams that have been placed on our hearts by something greater than us. The dream can supply a nation, the dream can inspire the next world leader or difference-maker. The dream has a purpose, the dream has potential, make the dream your reality. Dream Big.

The Big Dream has to come from within. In life when I began working on myself and working towards my dreams and goals personally and financially I realized that I did not Dream Big Enough. I achieved my dream home that I walked into at the age of 11. My mom's friend lived there. Her home was beautiful, and she was a strong self-willed woman, as I look back I bet she had the love of Jesus in her. She was her own woman. I walked into her home only once and said that time to her. If I ever live in Fremont this will be my home.

Amazingly after many years, I found myself after the long-suffering season in my journey that I was given my dream home.

My home life was in an uproar and chaos and confusion were going on all around me. I can remember crying before I went to the scheduled meeting to walk through the house. My two youngest kids both had been to court for something they really did. I had to let them stand on their own and begin making their own decisions. I don't know if you did it or not but these are the three choices the court is going to give you. This is what each of them means. I am not sitting with you in front of the judge, nevertheless I will be sitting right behind you. You are not alone. We as parents must prepare our children for real life. It is not all fun and games outside. It's dark and many many people enjoy the darkness because they are ashamed of their true character to be shown in the light. At some point in life especially after the age of 13, we have to decide to live for the Lord.

Setting your treasures in eternity instead of being influenced and misled into a life of destruction.

I praised, I prayed and I cried. I had a choice and the choice was hard, juggling a career just coming out of a marriage, kids well known by the probation officer, another daughter who had been violated by someone she trusted and I am learning my career while doing my career with no help and know that this career is a gift from God literally, so I can not quit. I had nothing, no one, this was my hometown. Where I grew up and graduated, ran the streets, and had my babies. My kids and my career, that's it. This was my dream home. I praised, I prayed, I cried. I wiped my face, put on my lip gloss and dressed for work. I made enough money, my credit was poor and I trusted God that he did not bring me this far to leave me. He told me a long time ago this was my house and it was. This was my Big Dream home. It was nothing but God, I toured the home and in every room, I thanked the Lord in advance for I knew that this was mine. I was going to be blessed with this house. I wasn't concerned about the credit check, the fact that I was number 149 to view the home. This was my house. There was only one black man who lived on this side of the street, and he lived with a white woman. I was the only black woman who lived in these homes on this side of the street. I did it. I made it, I worked hard and just trusted God. He is all I had, he is who I told my dream to. He heard my cries. He blessed me with this home. I did not have the credit score to qualify for the home, I did not have the rental history to qualify for the home and I did not have the money to qualify for the home. You can not tell me at not point in time when God wants to bless you he can and will bless you and nothing will stand in the way of that blessing. Trusting God is the best thing I ever did. He has never left me or forsaken me. He is who knows my true self and if you can be true in front and to him he can

69

show you your gifts and purpose and teach you his will for your life so that you may have peace and joy. I lived in my dream home for eight years. Everything happens for a reason, are you sober enough to hear the small voice of your intuition and seek the knowledge of Peace and Joy? Where is your treasure? Once you have been given the desires of your heart then what? I have had my dream home, I have had my dream car. I have met and dated my dream man, and I have experienced my fantasies and passions, once you have done all the things that you have dreamed of, then what? Once you earn all the material tangible things then what? This life I live, I live for Christ Jesus.

When there are no more fleshly desires then what? Do not get lost in the darkness just cause you can, remember "What is done in the Dark ALWAYS come to the Light." My Dream is Big. "My dream is Bigger than me, it's Bigger than you, but it's not Bigger than Us". - quote from a friend.

Generations:

The Genealogy of the human race is based on genealogy. We often wonder why the nose was blown off the Egyptian pyramids and in the early days, the movies portrayed people of color as white people or just disregarded the description of the race altogether as if we could not read. Oh, they tried to stop that as well. Why is the attack on people of color? They attacked people who were brown-skinned, took and purchased them from their homeland to filter the riches from it and built a land of darkness based on wealth and status, who you know and the darkness hid within. They attacked the yellow people wanting their drugs and influence their purchased power, The people of dark beliefs attack the people who are of a particular decent, or genealogy, to kill gas and burn as to extinct a race, similar to the savages who claim to discover a land that was inhabited with people who lived freely, shared freely to be deceived by darkness and destroyed. Genealogy of the family unit of a honey-skinned person, who speaks with a fast tongue, they are grounded in family and tradition. They worked hard and played only to be used to complete the menial task of cleaning and gardening to be used and paid little for their hard work and dedication. Once learn that they work hard and work together to be able to live the lives they only dream of once they arrive home, to learn that their land occupies a kingdom of heightened sense of calm and hyper that produces profits for all involved. The darkness then forms a way to gain and attack, build and destroy. Now the impact is being heard all over the world, the war of all wars, the Light against the Darkness, the Good against the Bad and the genealogy of the people. At some point in history, the wording was changed, it used to be the Jews, and Gentiles at what point did it become Black and White? What about the geology of a people is so important to go to such lengths to cover it up, hide it, and deceive people for the true explanation of what season we are in? It is Dark outside, find your light and develop it to shine bright, there are some people that can not see.

Generation is defined as A generation refers to all of the people born and living at about the same time, regarded collectively. It can also be described as, "the average period, generally considered to be about 20-30 years, during which children are born and grow up, become adults, and begin to have children."

71

Generation Names

- The Greatest Generation - born 1901-1927. ...

- The Silent Generation - born 1928-1945. ...

- The Baby Boomer Generation - born 1946-1964. ...

- Generation X - born 1965-1980. ...

- Millennials - born 1981-1996. ...

- Generation Z - born 1996-2012. ...

- Gen Alpha - born 2013 - 2025.

It is time to know who you are your purpose and God's will for your life. You are in a battle for your eternity for your Dream. Know your history and learn from your past. It was just preparation for your future. Knowing you can do all things through Christ who Strengthens you, means you have been given a path to gain understanding. Everyone learns differently and that is the purpose of the metaphors and stories so that individuals can relate on their own terms where they are at in their own journey. Each of us has gifts and talents that will bring us peace and joy. However many of us operate in our own power and then wonder why we are stressed, depressed and confused. We don't have to walk alone however in this day and age you must be careful to whom and what you are attached to. Not everything that looks good is good, happiness is not joy and chaos and confusion are not from God.

My Big Dream is to create a legacy for my children's children. When we first think of legacy, we go to inheritance and wealth that is passed down from generation to generation. That is what I am talking about however my wealth, legacy is more valuable than the monetary things of this world. I want to pass down integrity, morals, values and mostly love. I want them to know love, feel love and give love. Not to be afraid of love and to be open and honest with themselves. I want them to be who I am, not what I do but the truth to themselves that they do not have to put on a mask for anyone. Use their energy to do things that bring them joy and peace. I want each of them to have a purpose and move in purpose. I want them to be strong leaders in whatever field their gifts lead them to. I want them to remember the hugs from NaNa and to share them with those whom they love. I want them to be able to conquer the hard days like John Wick fighting for his life, I want them to place their treasure in heaven so that they may walk in peace on earth.

The dedication I put into breaking generational curses will help build a foundation for generations to come. The world is not the same, however the schemes of the enemy are. Know your enemy for he is battling the same God for your soul. Salvation can be in the Light or the Darkness. Just know if you choose darkness, it is torture and pain for eternity, no peace, no joy, just the destruction of the sin that you agree was worth nothing but giving up everything. You still have light, don't be afraid to let it shine, let it shine, let it shine.

It is amazing how you are told that the enemy seeks to kill and destroy and there a generations and generations of people that will still seek after the riches of this world to only seek to flaunt in front of others that are less fortunate or in a different stage in their journey. These people with whom many think they have it all, one thing I do not see is peace and joy. Do we really miss the fact that they say they can not sleep at night and they are overworked and they are a beck and call of a master or machine that the demands of fame and the reward of fortune are over whelming? Where your dream becomes a burden and the desire for a simple life outweighs the pleasure of silver and gold. Humility becomes bad and constant pressure becomes a way of life. You work hard to be more valued dead than alive. What is your legacy, what type of life are you leading? It will be your conversation at the end of the line, where you review your life, there will be ups and downs and decisions and consequences. There will be good and bad, there will be a judgment at the end of the line, and you will have decided to get with this or get with that. No matter who you are, what your skin color is, what language you speak. We will all be at the end of the line. What will be your story... What had happened would not be allowed. There will be no explanation, it is what it is. It will be standing on business as your thoughts, desires, actions, choices, and consequences play out in front of you. This is your story, your Dream. Did you quit halfway through, was the fight too hard? Did you even try? Did you call on the provider, the healer, the friend? Did you dream big enough? Will you be proud of your story as it is passed down from generation to generation? Are you a help or a hindrance? Your choice, your fruit. Your story. Your Dream.

My Grandpa was born of the silent generation. It shows in his character. I had the pleasure of knowing my Paw Paw John Will, was and he is from what they call the Greatest Generation. He was that Great! He brought his family from the South to the North and paved a foundation for them to become strong men. Providers and Protectors of their family. He was a Cornerstone in the Church built in the North. He broke generational curses from being a sharecropper in the South to becoming a planted industrialist in the foundry and paved the way for all of his boys to do the same. I also was blessed to have time with Madea, Huddles or Idell as some would call her. She too was from the Greatest Generation. She had a story where she was married at 13 had children and came up north to raise her family, she too from the South. She was a housewife and took care of the home and the kids. Her husband Buddy worked as an industrialist and Madea became a cornerstone of the church up north. With raised a family of girls who were strong career-minded, nurses, cooks, bus drivers and travellers. This Great Generation of my family produced a strong family generation that we grew up into. Holidays were the best just because we got to see and spend time with family. The atmosphere was always of love and peace, laughter and fun, music and dancing. The joy was there. We had gardens and barbecues, and we always had plenty and leftovers at times. We never ran out of things to drink or food to eat. You left with smiles and empowered with joy. This was the Greatest Generation.

The Silent Generation is my grandfather and I can see this. He enjoys company, he enjoys stories. He rarely states an opinion on anything. Says nothing but knows all. In his later years, he opened up more, as we were growing up he did not interfere or judge. He observed and I guess prayed. He walked in his own way, never around many or chased. He has always stood as his own man. My grams are from the same silent generation. As she speaks more about her childhood and youth, I see so much of her in me. She endured many things and never said a word, now that she has the excuse of getting older she just says whatever and it is educational, funny and cute. Things she was silent about for many years. She endured, he endured, they were silent.

My mother and I are from Generation X. This tells me a lot. This is when these people may have figured that if they control a generation two generations later they will get results of their programming. This is your black panther, introduce crack cocaine, feed them the drugs, destroy the black fathers, destroy the black homes. Introduction of

Hud, segregation and Martin Luther King Jr. to distract them from what we are really trying to achieve in destroying a race of people. They used segregation and the fight for equality to build and tear down the black man. Yes, we got in the house, wanting what others had, or fair treatment and then Martin found out the house was on fire. Leading people to destruction. They will help, however, it comes at a cost.

I too am a part of Generation X. I was able to experience the influence of our elders, what it was like to feel equal and not segregated and then to watch the growth of technology, the destruction of a people and the programming of depression, addiction and poverty mindset. The later part of Generation X still had choices. We watched the destruction of our parents with addiction, we took what was given to us for evil and by the introduction of Millennials, began providing homes, education, and support for those less fortunate. We began purchasing homes without the 30-year mortgage and gaining assets equal to that of the caucasian race without the interest attached. Generation X began breaking the addiction curses with the grace of God, people waking up in a day deciding no more and standing on it. Dads began to go back home, Single mothers began to work and provide and dependency on others was declining, or so we thought.

Once the recovery began and faith was walking, the phase changed. Children began making more than their parents and began to be influenced that Silver and Gold were more valuable than Jesus. The Bling Bling was a whole distraction to influence the passion of let's fix what's wrong in our hoods to glamorize the destruction of our own people. Looking from today back to that day, they knew the destruction was coming they were warning us in the interviews and the music. They knew hip hop was a tool to be used against a generation to influence them to reject what is good and cleave to what is bad. It was a well-orchestrated plan that would allow control of a whole generation. It was a plan of old which is why all of the old people are still sitting in the seats of influence. There is a reason that there is a process to salvation just like there is a process to fame and fortune. One offers worldly treasures the other offers treasures the world can not buy. The deception or manipulation of it is to believe or not to believe. Now that the war is here many of the warriors have fallen victim to the enemy and cover themselves in sheep's clothing while working for the wolf seeking to kill and destroy. It is not hard to understand the manipulation in thinking that you are weak if you are a sheep, forgetting the tail of the shepherd boy who defeated the giant. It had nothing to do with his build or occupation, it had to do with who he knew and believed in. A sheep would appear to the natural eye as a weaker vessel but is it? The sheep endures, peacefully, and provides protection (covering). Grace and Mercy cover the sheep for its defences is not much, however, the support of the herd is invaluable. This allows the herder to go after the lost sheep and the others to be disciplined enough to be managed in large quantities together in peace awaiting for the lost one to be found. It does not take much to devour or much courage to follow the pack to destruction, strength is in your will to stand alone, stand for your purpose, stand in patience, and stand on the business that will provide a return on investment, that has no expiration date. You will never walk alone. It will always be a blessing or lesson.

The Millennials were introduced and grew up with technology that would change everything that we now know. All things can be recorded and tracked. The whole goal is for the corporation to keep track of the employees while hiring CEOs to organize and ensure the tracking of the implantation of the influence to destroy and control a generation beyond parents or moral individual control. This is the end of children going to vacation bible school and doing Easter Speeches. This is the generation of knowledge of the world and worldly riches and not of the fear of Jesus returning soon. This is the generation of things, cars, crips and purses. This is the generation of confusion. Confusion thinking you know more than your elders and disrespecting your heritage to covet things that were never meant for you. Tommy Hilfigure, a well-known brand in the 90s stated that he did not make his clothing for people of color and did not want them to purchase them. Then, people of color thought, some went and purchased because he said not to. They just put money into the pockets of a known enemy. This is what we do every day when we follow behind the enemy who we know is praying for our downfall. Giving ammunition for the enemy to shoot us every time we open the door to sin. Think about it.

Millennials are the generation of kids from Generation X who were empowered by the enemy to call the authorities on their parents. There are some children in need of help and interference from a third party, no doubt and I am not talking about those situations. I am talking about the blatant situations of others out of envy, jealousy and pure evil that would call a third party on individuals to have their children taken from them or children to call authorities on their parents so they can have their way. Encouraging kids to have power over their parents created a generation of undisciplined children who have been corrupted to the point that the sin they were born into has not been corrected and grown them into full demons that walk the earth with destruction and chaos, parties, addictions, lies, gossip, humiliation, and everything dark to grow within. Men are now lovers of

Men, due to the example of a strong black man who has been emasculated to the point that men want to be "Bad Bitches' ' not even Strong Women. Girls want to be "Thug boys' ' not even a strong man. There will be people who question their sexuality and will go before God with their explanation or review their story of why things are the way they are. However, there are some that are just going along with the sin that has built up in them. How the rights of a choice of sexuality that you were given, becomes more important than the choice of salvation is above me. It is what it is. Some people are pretending to go along with the trend or hide their insecurities. Fake people will not be allowed in Heaven. People who wish badly on other people will not be allowed in Heaven. People who gossip and lie will not be doing that in Heaven. People who sleep with the same sex will not be doing that in Heaven. People who kill people will not be allowed in Heaven. People who idolize and put things or people before God will not be doing that in Heaven. People who are not authentically themselves will not be walking around Heaven. Heaven is said to have no more pain, no more grief so how can you enter if your insides are filled with bitterness, unhappiness, Inverness, lust and envy? You need to develop a mentality of I am in this world but not of this world. My treasure is in Heaven and I am going to practice living and preparing my life for my eternal home, full of peace and joy. It won't be easy, however, the review of my story will show me trying. Millennials were born into confusion, confusion of the transformation of generations, from family to relatives to influence to destruction only to be used to rebuild what has been broken. Light overcomes the darkness. Greater is he that is within me, than he that is in the world. Now how to teach a generation that there is a war going on and they have been used as pawns in the game of life, the supernatural is upon us and those who can see, see.

79

Jett James

Those who don't seek out the understanding to know on this day who you serve. Dream Big!

This Generation Z is a computer chip. They are programmed to look at their phones and be influenced by what they see, with no depth or substance to the influence. There is no question of why. Just follow, just do. This is the generation of the crate challenge, set up just to see how gullible people are. You see people doing it, you see people falling, you know they are hurting themselves and yet people are willing to try it for no reward. Why? And the real question is where did everyone get all those crates from? I know people did not go pay $7-$10 for a crate that will serve no purpose after you attempt a challenge that pays no reward. A sucker move, cause anyone can tell that that is not a good idea. A generation that blindly follows the trend. A generation that flashes top brand names that already make money to lower their standards and allow black people, you know those people of color that build this country on their backs, literally, mothered the children of the forefathers, ploughed their fields, and invented the technology only to be stripped away of their dignity and manhood. It is disappointing to know that people fought for freedom and that a generation has been deceived to give it all back by the lack of growth and support of people of the same color or predicament.

This is the generation that fully falls for them against us and us against them, divided by color, or sex when the real battle is spiritual. How can a generation that has not been shown or taught about the light of the spiritual things, but influenced by the dark distractions of what this corrupt world has to offer? When the light and knowledge of real men have been replaced by feminine boys to influence that power and fame are more than integrity and morals. An imaginary photo of people in high places supporting you only to set you up and take what

80

is rightfully yours. This generation has to deal with grooming, the influence of having this, you must do this, you must do this until it is uncomfortable and then you need to do it some more. Taking the very essence of what makes you, you and leading to you a dark place a sunken place that you are unable to even look at yourself in the mirror. This generation, this is their life, this is their experience unless you show them different. Love stories are not the same, they are sex stories and the sex stories tell you stories of the same sex as if a man and woman together in loyalty and love is a sin and partnership and profit is what relationships are built on. We must do better.

We grew up on music that was called Rhythm and Blues, Pop, Real Hip Hop. Not this water-down version with no emotion or no feeling. that is called soulless. When you encounter people who don't care, they can take life, don't support the life they created, they are empty inside. Can dish out pain as if it is macaroni and cheese on Thanksgiving, their soul has been locked up and tainted. Salvation, many are called few are chosen we all can be forgiven. We forgive so we can be forgiven. Many Sins are done in the dark and when they come to the light they cause many people shame and depression, unforgiveness of self. The real question is if you may regret it once the results are known why do it? I prayed for a son, I prayed for an athletic son. My son's

father came to marry my cousin. My then-husband took full responsibility for my son. My son was loved, beyond DNA, rumours, and the opinion of others. Due to the choices and decisions made. I do not regret the choice that I made one night to lay with a man I was not in a relationship with, the result was a very athletic baby boy that had characteristics of three people, DNA from us that produced the sperm and egg that created a seed to grow into the embryo and eventually produced my handsome child. How can any of that be in regret? The damage we cause by our choices and not being honest with our children can leave them feeling some kind of way. The next time you go to talk badly about your child's parents, remember you were the one who made the choice to lay with that person and you should express the feelings and thoughts that you had at the time of conception not at the time of heartbreak and disappointment. That is your child's other half of DNA. God does not make mistakes and children are here for a reason. I was gifted with mine to love, train and direct, at 13 teach them about choices for then they will stand before the altar of God alone. The Rn B music provided a healing that "Scooch Over" just can not heal. " If You Think You're Lonely Now, A House is not a Home, Not gon Cry, We Belong Together, After the Pain, Happy Feelings, A Ribbon in the Sky.. " these songs can hit your soul in a way that can bring tears to your eyes and healing to your heart. You can praise through the rough times until one day you feel no more pain, you have the strength to get up. You can fight another day. You feel, you process, you heal. Now the influence is nothing. Physical, lust. They do not tell you until you have made love with true feeling and emotion you miss the whole point of sex and the gift and passion within it. When you feel a person and your bodies combine, if you are feeling a feeling of love between each other, passion, loyalty, and trust where you open yourself up to accept that person you have not climaxed. You can fake it, if you do you still come out unfulfilled. Giving yourself to everyone and anyone is a weakness, strong people are choosy lovers. Weak people have sex, we need more strong people who are not afraid to be in love, more aware of the reward of intimacy and fornication. It's not easy, that is why the Lord will work on you until the day of his return. Will your story show that you are trying?

I watch Generation Z stay to themselves, a new version of the silent generation. They are knowledgeable but each is to their own passion and desire. They nestled into the video games and tick-tocks that influence their life. They are living in a virtual reality not focused on reality. They do not care much about going out into the real world and having real experiences. They value the time from when they wake up until they go to sleep in a virtual reality of what they feel is living better than their elders.

Gen Alpha has been given the power to change their sex before they have sex or develop to the point of puberty. The parents that go along with this narrative somehow miss the fact that if your child's sex is changed and they are making these types of decisions for themselves, you too will stand with them before God. Do not miss the instruction to train a child as they should go, when they are grown they will not depart from this. There will be some who will question their sexuality. There will be some parents that will have to deal with it. If God brings you to it He will bring you through it. While I am responsible for you, me and my house will serve the Lord. When you are grown and providing for yourselves then you can have power over your life. Parents need to get back to parenting. No, the deceptions and what the world is telling you are not always designed to get you to the promised land, but to deceive you into thinking wrong is good, good is wrong, bad is good, and good is bad. This is a trick of the enemy. That is why you have that small voice that always provides you with a choice. The hard part is going against the crowd or what you see, and having faith in what you know. What can not be seen is faith. Our conversations have to be different, we are dealing with different approaches to the same problem. We have silenced our voices. It is time to speak up.

This life I live I live for Christ Jesus who saved my soul. I do what I do so my children's children can too have a chance at salvation. We are under attack and we need to Armor up for War. What side are you fighting on?

When the Chemo fluids were pumping through my body the cancer and everything else was being killed and forced out of my body. The time of isolation and sickness removed people who were attached to me for all of the wrong reasons. The time allowed me to see who was there for me and prayed and supported me in my needest time and also the intentions of those whom I have held close. Isolation is a time to reflect, to learn and grow yourself. The time of fasting and praying working on your own character without the influence of others is the most important time. This time is needed and should be placed as a very important part of life balance. You hear of people who go to the prayer closet or people who say I need time alone.

That is time to reflect and adjust, seek and correct if needed. We were all born into sin and we all fall short of the Glory of the Lord. However, if you seek the Kingdom of God and spend time with you He can lead you to the land of righteousness and salvation. Only through him can He forgive your sins and teach you how to forgive yourself. Learning to forgive yourself will allow you to have peace within and forgiving others will allow the Father in Heaven to forgive you. On the other side of Cancer, I became a new person, being down for a year, allowed me to not sin in lustful ways, it allowed me time to speak and seek salvation on a deeper level. When all the Sin was flushed from my body it allowed space for the righteousness of the Lord to come in and provide me with wisdom and knowledge on how to navigate this new life in Christ. The life I live, I live for God, thy spirit is good, thou art my God lead me to the land of uprightness. You can not put new wine in old wineskins, the skins will burst. Empty your sins so you can be filled with the light of God. Faith without works is dead. The first step to salvation is the first step. Not the elevator, the stairs. What are the steps to your Big Dream that can be easily achieved by knowing your purpose? Be Strong, Be Confident, and Be Encouraged to take the first Step to make your Dreams a Reality.

A Big Dream must and has to include a higher power. That reward of satisfaction that you receive when you can see the reality of your dreams come to pass from your dedication and belief to keep going. To see a way out of no way. When your faithfulness shows the vision of the glimpse that you received a long long time ago. The faith of walking where you can not see to see. Walking forward in uncomfortable places around uncomfortable people, then you can look back to reference those experiences that allowed you to grow in character and knowledge. To know what is for you is to know what you are not gonna do... What I am not going through again, what I am not going to tolerate. To know you are strong enough to walk away because you like yourself and enjoy your own company. Your energy is not for everyone, yet everyone will be affected if it is light. The darkness blends with an individual, Dream Big.

The Big Deam is the quiet dream that only you and God know about. That dream where no one outside of yourself knows the passion of your heart. That Dream that you can say only you and God knew this is what you wanted. I mentioned I had an experience where I looked around and stated I did not dream big enough. I was able to experience the small mind of dreams that I had, the Big Dream is the dream that God has purposed for me. I dream of being able to sit in that purpose and confidently speak about it and the outside world is unable to even cross the doorstep of accessing me due to I am surrounded by defenders in the spirit that can identify anything that would attempt to come up against the purpose of my destiny, my Big Dream. Those answered prayers that can only be explained by my conversation with God and now that I review my journey I am so Blessed to say I saw you God, I did not know it then but I know it now. Seeing the Big Dream is more than material things and things.

It is the dream of eternity, of working on being ready until his return. If you haven't noticed, many of the things in life are a repeat of things that were before. Things, jobs, families, and marriage are at times more valued than peace, prosperity, and joy. We at times need to long for things to journey to the purpose and experience to be able to stand firm in who we were created to be. When you know that you are gifted to do a thing, I don't know how or why I am so good at this or that or this or that captures your interest and I enjoy doing it, it is not like work for me, but can be hard work for others. That is a gift, something that can lead you to develop your purpose. Everything happens for a reason. It really does, good bad, petty or ugly.

Peace, Prosperity and Joy are my big dreams. To live life working towards righteousness each day. Working towards being stronger and faithful in my walk with Christ. The Lord knows what I need and he knows where I still need to learn. If I walk uprightly there is no shame or condemnation in anything that I do. Waking in the truth means there is no lie to hide. I have to stand before what I believe about myself, I have to stand through trials and tribulations, and I have to stand on the business of me. I am my Big Dream seeking to make the vision that is placed in my heart a reality that was only made possible by the Grace of God. Some will go, some will not. I see when you do the work to make dreams a reality and go after what you want with or without the support of your peers, it's rare. Some come up with reasons why you can't. That is why the Big Dream is personal, they don't see the vision because it is not their vision. You can do what you put your mind to especially if it is what you were supposed to do. At some point in time, the people stopped dreaming about becoming president, and settled for being a thug, without knowing the true meaning of what that was when it was. The definition of that was changed too.

Our surroundings have influenced us not to dream but to covet, our surroundings at times have influenced money of joy, power over peace, manipulation over truth. There is a process to get to the other side of anything, good or bad. Too much energy is being used to fuse the darkness and the deception of not knowing that you have a light that makes you an individual, not invalid. If everyone is the same and does the same and seeks the same that makes them the same, invalid. Individuals are who the one true God created us to be, yes there was Cain and Abel. Darkness Cain seeks to kill and destroy. Light Able, praises and shows glory to God above all else. That side or this side. Life is a lesson to grow each day, how you choose to live that life is up to you. If you are experiencing a lot of drama, frustrations, stress, chaos, and confusion that means there is darkness around you. If you want peace, prosperity and joy you must seek it. Everyone's journey is different and some journeys may cross, in everything is a lesson and a blessing. If you do not learn the lesson, those experiences you keep having over and over, you will keep experiencing the lesson over and over. When you learn the lesson and apply it to your life it is your life, the blessings, the results or receiving the desires of your heart. Gratefulness is the only response, what are you thankful for? If you can not find anything to be thankful for, you may need to really search yourself and ask what is important to you, and what you want to achieve in life. If your only answer is money, you vibrate low. There is so much more out there.

Money is a thing, it is not Everything. Dream Bigger.

Once you achieve all of the things you want in life, what do you do next? Do you sink into your earthly desires of drugs party and rock and roll? That gets old, you get old. Then what? Will everyone be stuck in a cycle of depression and desperation in a meaningless life wandering around as a zombie due to failure to even try to be or evolve into more? The only limit on you is the limit you place on yourself. There is more and there is light there is better you just have to want it. That is that seeking .. seeking knowledge on how to navigate in life in the good and bad times, the knowledge to seek to grow in fast seasons, long seasons, big reasons or small reasons, the lifetime that makes up the wholeness in you or continue to walk around broken due to your too weak to do the work. The trick of the enemy is telling you it is hard to be evil when in reality that is the easiest thing to do. When you go with the crowd no one is really going against you until you stop following the crowd. When you stop following the crowd they see the greatness grow in you and generate the energy they have within themselves to go against you and hard is fighting the thoughts and energies that you were once a part of. There is a war going on and you will need to decide where you're going to stand. It will not be easy, fight for you. You're worth it. This was fun, go for more, there is more out there for you. Purpose.

Know what yours is Dream Big!

The steps of a Righteous Man are ordered. If you are too big to follow you will never be Big enough to Lead. The truth will set you free, Good is not evil and evil is not Good.

The deception of this world is that the heightened sense of a man-made drug is the best feeling in the world that causes you to bypass your self-inhibitions, morals and values and lower your energy to live in what is dark.

To have your Big Dream you have to be willing to break the chains that are holding you back from achieving what is proposed to be achieved. These chains are usually visualized in nature. I am unable to do this because of money, because of support, because of this and that. Breaking chains of nature is moving differently to breaking chains like working more hours and dedicating some of your income to making your dream a reality. Faith without works is dead or the people who know you and surround you do not see you, but what about those who do not know you and those who have been waiting to see what you have depending on what you can provide, what about those outside of your comfort zone, those who are your people. God shares his plans for a reason, it is up to you to act on that reason with or without the support of those you think should support you. It's bigger than them, it's bigger than you. Faith without works is dead. The chain link can be this or that it is your chain and it is you who can work towards breaking the chains that hold you anchored in a life that you have outgrown. You can do anything you put your mind to, what natural differences can you do each day to help get you closer to your Big Dream?

The Spiritual or Supernatural chains take a different approach or look into yourself to develop the character that you truly are. Getting to know yourself processing the pain and leaving it there. Forgiving and moving on, Forgetting yet learning discernment. I can forgive you and I can forget, I also can discern that if you stung me once I will not allow you to sting me again. You can not get that close. I did not lose you, you lost me. The friend I thought you were, you weren't. When I learn the lesson I move on, when I try to teach you the lesson, I am only wasting my time. My business is about me and my relationship with my saviour is more important than anything, if you are not for me you are against me. I will not be stung again. I can see that coming. The chain is broken and you have nothing to hang on to. We were, we used to be and we are, however, that access has been broken. We must be able to respect each other enough to know your choices are for you and my choices are for me. You choose to walk in darkness and are okay with your life being an eternity of hell for temporary riches. Reminds me of the mindset of I am not going to work all year because I don't want to make enough money to be placed in a higher tax bracket because I am okay with receiving a once-a-year large lump sum check that I spend as soon as I get it. On vacations, cars I can not afford, clothing to prove to other poor people I can obtain. Some have the smarts to invest in a temporary business but they have not developed the commitment to stay within the hard times. What comes easy goes easy, what you work hard for you will cherish or value more. That one check once a year can be a help and a hindrance. Your perspective and self-progress will show the direction you are going in. When you make decisions are you making decisions according to what you want the outside or people to perceive about you? Are you doing it for the people? Or can you say this is my dream, I am doing this to better myself, for me, or for my family where the reason has nothing to do with anyone but for the Glory of God? There is a difference.

Let's call it the chain "for the people". Many of us are caught up in the for the people Cuban link chain. The rope chain is called "for the bag", you know when your only goal in life is to have money to show off to people. The diamond chain called "for the fame" you move so people can see you and follow you kind a self worship making yourself a God. These chains are the most coveted or what people want, the things, chains with no substance or value. These chains are as superficial as a golden globe or an Emmy..if you do not get paid for these statues why have them, why covet them, why worship them? It may be a chain of manipulation to have you worship something other than the one true God through Jesus Christ. If the dark links can provide things in the darkness just imagine what the superficial glory of the Light and the things that God has prepared for you. Just like the script is written in the entertainment world, the streets of Heaven are paved with Gold. My dainty gold chain only has to hold on to the word of God and though it may be thin and dainty the bond is stronger than all. All chains that are not of God, through my Lord Jesus Christ. Break every Chain. No more depression, no more grief, no more poverty, no more hate, no more darkness. The light lives within me, the dream of being a light, the proof and testimony that you can break every chain.

In the realization and the pursuit of your Big Dream, you will have Judas among you. In dealing with and identifying these, you need to think about the word that says love your enemies, love conquers all, pray for your enemies, and keep your enemies close. God rains on the just and the unjust, my God loves you like he loves me, you just have to seek him and His righteousness. Achieving the big dream is not easy, it will take time Patience, long-suffering, tests and trials, and tribulations. Facing life at this time of lifeing is happening for everyone, beyond the money, beyond the mask, beyond the material, there is a valuable dream within each and every one of us. We have been conditioned to go after what you see, the Gangster Rap, drug trade, and Bling Bling, the whole process was a distraction from the path of individualism. You see more people than individuals. To give you a visual I went to a vibrant lounge in a popular city and it was packed full of all types of people but the same people. We could count the number of men who did not have a bald head and beard easier than we could count the ones who were individuals. This place had hundreds of people in it. The visual gave me a better understanding of people vs individuals. Everyone has their own journey, however, how do you have a life to your full potential or to your big dream if you are following the influence of something or someone else that is not the essence of you? Mind, body and soul. With that is a spirit. That is the human make-up. How are you managing your mind, what are you looking at daily, and what do you spend most of your time doing? It's your time, it's your dream, it's your reality. Are you living your dream? Your mind runs your body, how do you see your body, what is your own opinion of your body? Is that opinion of yourself positive or negative? Why? How do you encourage yourself? Do you have emotions? Do you hate? Do you love it? Are you mad? Do you hold a grudge? Do you smile? Do you know who you are without any outside voices? Can you sit in the quiet and listen to yoursoul? Wisdom, where are you smart? What do you need to do to be smarter, and wiser?

What are you interested in? What do you like to do? Who do you want to be? What bringsyou peace? The Big Dream? What is your dream? What is your treasure? Do you live to please the world or do you set your treasures higher? The Big Dream is realizing something will need to fall away, the test is to remain who you are and understand where they are. Who are you to judge, who am I to judge? That is for you and that is you, I love you however I will be over here. Be slick as a snake and gentle as a dove.

They can slither in the yard, My God is in the fire with me and goes before me. He covers me on all sides with his holy armor, weapons may form but they will not prosper. I have a Big Dream and the battles may get harder and stronger, trust in the Lord. I know he prepares a path for me. Help me to remain humble at all times. My dream is Big and I know he is more than I could ever ask. He needs me to be ready and standing firm in His holy word. Help me to always seek you first in all things. Thank you. It is your haters who promote you without you even knowing it. Embrace and pray for your enemies for they are children of God. The battle is not with flesh and blood. Dream Big,it's your Dream.

In the big dream at one time all little girls wanted to grow up and get married. The conversation used to be this is how I would like my wedding and this is how I would like my home. Nowadays if you listen how many individuals can tell you this is my goal and This is my dream without it being something outlandish like I want to go to Dubai or go see all this man-made glory in the middle of the desert in a place that states we have rules, and you will pay us to enjoy what appears as luxury at a high price for the gram. If you live in that lifestyle and you can afford your luxuries and it is a blessing I am not speaking negatively in any way, I like nice stuff as well. Yet in all of its gloriousness the Peace and Joy from within is far more valuable. No matter what you can afford.

The inner longing for family comes from creation, we have been bamboozled into thinking that being independent and without fellowship and companionship is the way of life. We have been influenced to lose the respect for the family unit and ORDER of the home. We have been manipulated to think a side chick is a win and a wife is weak. So deceived to think a strong man shows his feminine side and a weak man stands with integrity and morals. A generation has been brainwashed to think that scamming and being flashy drinking and drugs are the coolest things ever and if you are living this dark lifestyle of disrespect lies and falsehood you are winning and succeeding. Make it make sense really. The temporary win is not more valuable than your individual talent or gift. See this is the part where people are seeing bad good and good bad.

That is not good. Fact If everyone who is doing wrong knows that they are doing wrong, then they want to excuse their behavior in the loss of material things, drinking and drugs. Oh and let's not forget the sex. The illusion that having orgies and sleeping with multiple people makes you cool or admired or desired is a trick your mind is playing on you. In the end, the enemy will look at you and say you chose to do this, you knew it was wrong and destroying your life. The illusion is you being around so many people thinking this is success and in reality, you are the one losing out the most. If you wasted your talents, in the end, whose fault is that? We all have a sad story, something we had to go through. It is a part of life. The integrity and values is the foundation of who you are as a person. If you're loose in the caboose and disrespectful to all who oppose your low-vibration point of view, don't be mad at the person who decides to push through and go after all this world has to offer them. Yes, there will be bad days,but when you learn not to complain and put trust in what is real, what is true, and what are you eventually the good days will out way the bad days. There is a reason that many personal stories that are told involve some sort of trauma or tragedy. To get anywhere there will be some sort of longsuffering. One thing I think my culture fails to realize is that our culture and gifts are powerful, so we have been misled to believe in the material physical things of this world. We are a supernatural being with supernatural abilities. Gifts Talents, wisdom and knowledge are instilled within us. We are becoming and our time is coming and we will be told that mental illness is real, we will be led to think we are crazy when we realize that It does not have to be dark outside, that is not success. It is our culture to want to fellowship and come together and become one, if you notice the attack is to ensure that does not happen. Gifts and Talents, no one can deny that R. Kelly is a very talented man.

Opinions can and will be made about his character, which in that has meaning. In reality, his journey is his, we are speaking on talent gifts. He is said not to be able to read but can produce, write and excel at his career to the heights that he has. If you were in the 90's there was and is no denying R. Kelly, talent, gifts. Be it as it may, the poise and precision that President Obama and Lady Michelle Obama gave to gifts and talents, though it may seem as it is, that was not easy to be in such a position. In the reality of things. The misconception of the family is rooted and has destroyed the Black Community, however the Culture is still in tack. Those who do not value what it is will see destruction, will be introduced and not be feared. When fear is all you can offer, you do realize you have no power once that person overcomes that fear. It is a new day. It is a new dream. Identify your gifts, your talents and even while your life is lifinnnn you will be living. Living the Big Dream and identifying Peace and Joy from within and happiness with you and your choices.

So from the beginning women, were created from Adam (which is probably why there are so many feminine men- y'all done kept the rib for your helpmate and your eve). Hey don't be sensitive or"offended" that is what you chose to do. I can laugh, if my wig fell off you would laugh at me and I could not be mad because I chose to wear that wig that day. It is what it is. So we as women were created to crave family and motherhood, we were given wombs to carry babies.

This is how we were made up. In this world today they want us to believe that it is okay to change your sex and it is okay for grown men to traffic children.The impression that it is okay to take someone's life and that makes you respected is such a misconception of everything integrity and morals stand for, not to even state a straight sin per the 10 commandments. Those are easy rules to follow, well at least a basis of a moral compass. The misconception of what sex is and made for. I have compassion upon a whole generation who has never made love or experienced love and the amazing aurora of what love really truly is. It is just sex and let me let you in on a secret, sex is not all that great. Yeah for the moment, however, love lingers. Love heightens the intercity of two people coming together. The ideology of having multiple partners and jumping from person to person is a sign of insecurity. A strong person values commitment and works towards becoming a better person, not a worse dark ugly deceivious person. It does not make sense. Family communities have been destroyed by the basic person being misled on a path of destruction disguised as fortune and fame. All of this leads you to the lake of fire and the acceptance of temporary fame. Your goal is to be strong and desired and the enemy's goal is to distract you from the real vision with this "reality" vision until you miss the purpose of your gifts and talents that you never watered or took the time to evolve.

I never dreamed of building a home or having a home of my own. However, I see myself in many places doing the things my heart desires. Everyone has a vision and a path that was predestined for them before the creation of time. Each and every one of us has a purpose, a gift and a talent. All of us have integrity, and values and know right from wrong. We thought we were having fun in the dark in our secrets in our trickery, however in this new reality you are the light, you are the one who made someone's day, you are the one that learned how to sleep at night and you are the one who became better than you were yesterday. Calculate how you spend your twenty-four hours each day and in that how much of that is just for you. Be Better, Do Better, Dream Big.

We as women were designed to be a help mate, to be united with another and to be helpful to make it whole. The two imperfect people become one when a man and a woman are united together in union and believe in a true bond, when two are together they are powerful. A couple will be more powerful than an individual if they agree and believe together. Their energy becomes one, just like people who come together for the same cause, it allows a more powerful energy to come and achieve unity in togetherness. Unity is a good thing, we have been led and shown nothing but division and destruction since the beginning of time.

People can disagree, and discuss, without anger or malice. When things are done in love, that is strength, when you attack out of anger that is weaker, because you have yet to gain the strength to conquer your emotions. However, you do have that power. Marriage is a good thing if it is done with respect to what that union is and should be. Yes, things happen and people grow apart, however, they grow together as well. My grandparents have been together and married for 70 years. What a blessing, through the good and the bad, sickness and health, kids, grandkids, great-grandkids, and great-grandkids, with love and loyalty enduring the test of time. Many have houses, big mansions and high-rise apartments, but a home is more than the flash. A home is where your heart is, where the embrace of a hug is more valuable than the name-brand purse you carry. A home where you feel peace, and can rest and the joy of a home-cooked meal as the fragrance fills the air. Let us not forget where we come from. Sharecroppers were manipulated to work for small wages and yet still managed to create generations to come of their lineage in making the best out of what life had to offer. Some men in some cases took care of two homes and two families without missing a step, it is the reality of life. However, do know the strong man, who built families, and provided homes and for those families that he was the head of, the leader of. His castle and he is the King. His house, His home, his family and his own. Now more men want to be queens or wear skirts in a relationship because women have become so bold in their stature that it is hard to humble them into obedience to the order of how things should be. We have been confused to eliminate our power from within. We all have gifts and talents and Big Dreams. The distractions are real.

Finding yourself will be essential to achieving your Big Dreams. Knowing who you are and setting boundaries and limits on your pursuit, not of happiness but the installation of joy. The joy that is with in needs to rest on the knowledge that this is who I am and to know that is who you are.

We can seek out counselling and tactics that can develop our character to seek who we really are. There may be giants, obstacles, experiences, and chains that are holding us back and we need to process and move past the things we have overcome and grown through. Many of us hold on to pain and hurt and dwell in that season, and then wonder why bitterness and grudges have led to a life of complaining and gossip. We can move past all of that. We can heal. In healing, you learn yourself and how to protect yourself in developing your purpose. Everyone goes through storms it's how you manoeuvre in the midst of the thunder and lightning that develops your character in becomes your greatest self. We are individuals and everyone is created with a purpose and our own journey. Find who you are and seek to develop the character to be able to live in your Big Dream.

Along with everything that we dream for in life, many times the finances and things are first for those who wish they have and long for, many have chosen to lead masses to destruction on a pre-planned agenda to lead all to a drastic end. Some work on their body we faced influences of eating disorders and over eating, and changing the DNA or the God Given blessing in becoming the individual you were created to be. In many of these physical desires of willingness to go to extremes to achieve the approval of masses of people who do not or desire to even know who the real you is. The weight of the pressure to please people and compromising your Big Dream can cause harm to your mind, body and soul. The emotional essence of what makes each of us is not the same. The effect of pain, happiness, love and hate impacts our emotional being. The large push of mental illness and processing the traumas that life introduces to us is important to fellowship in releasing the everyday pressures of life. The outside has become so engrossed in the destruction of people that no one is taking the time to focus on helping to repair the internal, the things that are unseen. The bullying, the abuse, the lies, the gossip, the grief and the many other things that we hold inside. The time no one clapped or you heard and felt how those closest to you really feel about you. When you realize that you are not appreciated as much as you thought. Where family and friends pray for your downfall and celebrate your losses or when you slip into the darkness. These are the circumstances where our emotional or spiritual selves are being developed and our character is created. It is the easy road to follow what you have seen and create a representative of yourself. The representative is what you want people to see, how you move to create a character that is not really you, but the person that you think or feel those you are in front of want to see. Being you strongly, and emotionally takes work and confidence to walk in those uncomfortable places and face your fear, pain or abuse that trauma causes you to shut off and close up. Some people close up these areas and remember them no more, some create clouds of bitterness, and grudges, holding the pain, or trauma hostage and allowing it to grow and harbour space in their heart and mind that causes darkness and some spots in that individual's character. However, there are some who will go to the extent of processing that trauma to heal and gain the freedom of their life. This is facing what it is that so easily ensnares you and processing, the pain, the abuse, and the trauma to a place of healing and power where it no longer affects your character and the true person you are growing into. This process is not easy and it causes you to humble yourself in ways that only can develop you into the person you were really created to be. We make plans and we work to execute them. In the process of life, we all were created for a purpose and our natural gifts work into the grand scheme of things and how we are supposed to live. Peace and Joy is something that is within and can not be taken away unless you give it away. In order to achieve Peace and Joy you must work on those emotional traumas, pains, and hurts that have you chained to the past, chained to the darkness in order to grow into your best self. The Big Dream involves you becoming your best self so when you achieve all that is meant for you have been prepared to handle God's blessing responsibly. If you're in tune with yourself you will see the journey laid before you leading you to the purpose for your life. You, We, Us were all created for something and the wealth and the value of the intent of this life lies within not on what you can put on. The confusion of entertainment labelled reality has misled the masses into a state of purgatory where they have no sense of life or death, heaven or hell. In reality, as we watch all of this darkness unfold around us in the influences and deception of common sense, we can strongly come to the conclusion, that since we know there is dark (they are showing us and telling us every day) We can be Confident and have Faith in the Light, knowing it can and will pierce through any cloud. The greatness of the light comes from within, where your wealth is stored. Your wealth is for you and there is no need to covet or seek after anyone else's. Your dream is yours, your dream at the smallest moments is Big. It is the small steps you take and the commitment you make to continually grow that will be sure to have you achieve. DreamBig.

What If...

What if your testimony could change the world What if your testimony could save souls

What if your testimony could encourage people of all nationsWhat if your testimony could prompt change

What if your testimony could give hope What if your testimony could show away

What if your testimony could be exactly what the world needs to hear today

What if was a fifth We would all be drunk

(Natural)

What if can be Supernatural

What if I Dreamed Big and it all came true

What if I could tell you exactly thus saith the Lord on what to doWhat if my faith and works brought positive results

What if my spirit brings peace in the world throughout

What if there can be possibilities of things we can not see

What if stands between our faith of what can and could, should and shall beLet thy will be done.

Could've = Could Have Would've = Would Have Should've = Should Have

When your time comes you stand at account for your life. Remember that the could haves will be represented, the would haves will be explained and the should haves will be shown. So as you make choices to live this gift we have been given called life, know that forgiveness is real. Each day is a new start and your Big Dream is achievable. It's your choices that allow you to Dream Big.

In order to achieve your big dream you will need to have confidence in your vision in your direction and in the midst of your giants. You can be all that you desire to be if you put in the work and effort your reward will be great. The big dream is more than fame and fortune, it is more than material things. The Big Dream develops your character to become all you were created to be, working towards the goal of righteousness and persevering through the tests and trials to victory.

The Lord said to Gideon, " You have too many warriors with you. If I let y'all of you fight the Midianites, the Israelites will boast to me that they saved themselves by their own strength. (Judges 7:2) God reduced Gideon's soldiers from 32,000 to 300. We must recognize the danger of fighting in our own strength. We can be confident of victory against life's challenges and temptations only if we put our confidence in the Lord God and not in ourselves.

But the one who rules in heaven laughs. The Lord scoffs at them. (Psalm 2:4) Pride and power cause nations and leaders to rebel against God and they try to break free of him. But God laughs because any power they have comes from Him, and He can also take it from them. We need not feat the boasts of tyrants- they are in God's hands and will be judged by Him.

God is our refuge and strength, always ready to help in times of trouble. So we will not fear when earthquakes come and the mountains crumble into the sea. Let the ocean roar and foam. Let the mountains tremble as the waters surge! (Psalm 46:1-3) God is our refuge even in the midst of total destruction. He is not merely a temporary retreat; He is our eternal refuge and can provide strength in any circumstance.

"O Sovereign Lord," I said, " I can't speak for you, I am too young". The Lord replied " Don't say I am too young," for you must go wherever I send you and say whatever I tell you, and don't be afraid of the people. For I will be with you and protect you. I, the Lord have spoken! (Jeremiah 1:6-8) We should not allow feelings of inadequacy to keep us from obeying God. He will always be with us. If God gives you a job to do, He will provide all you need to do it.

So at day break, the apostles entered the Temple, as they were told, and immediately began teaching. When the high priest and his officials arrived, they convened the high council – the full assembly of the elders of Israel. Then they sent forth apostles to be brought from the jail for trial. (Acts 5:21) . When we are convinced of the truth of Christ's resurrection and have experienced the presence and power of the Holy Spirit, we will also have the confidence to speak out for Christ.

He did this so people would repent of their sins and be forgiven.

And my message and my preaching were very plain. Rather than using clever and persuasive speeches, I relied only on the Holy Spirit. (1 Corinthians 2:4) Effective Preaching results from studious preparation and reliance on the work of the Holy Spirit.

Jett James

This is what the scriptures mean when they say:" No eye has seen, no ear has heard,

And no mind has imagined what God

Has prepared for those who love HIM." (1 Corinthians 2:9)

Until the Holy Spirit comforts and guides us knowingly the wonderful and eternal future that awaits us gives us hope and courage to press on in this life, to endure hardship, and to avoidgiving into temptation. This world is not all there is. The best is yet to come. Dream Big!

For Other Information

Thank you for your time. I pray that this book has provided insight and encouragement in this new season of life.

Feel Free to contact me at jett.james@ymail.com for fellowship. I look forward to hearing from you! Be Encouraged and Dream Big.

www.ingramcontent.com/pod-product-compliance
Lightning Source LLC
LaVergne TN
LVHW052034080426
835513LV00018B/2313